The Dog Ate My Planner

Tales and Tips
from an Overbooked Life

Carmen,
Don't let the
dog eat your planner!
And keep pushing to get the
word out about your
wonderful book. I
certainly will.

Pat

The Dog Ate My Planner

Tales and Tips
from an Overbooked Life

PAT SNYDER

Illustrations By Michael H. Whiting

TWO HARBORS PRESS

Minneapolis, Minnesota

Two Harbors Press
212 3rd Avenue North, Suite 290
Minneapolis, MN 55401
612.455.2293
www.TwoHarborsPress.com

ISBN - 978-1-935097-26-6
ISBN - 1-935097-26-1
LCCN - 2009903300

Book sales for North America and international:
Itasca Books, 3501 Highway 100 South, Suite 220
Minneapolis, MN 55416
Phone: 952.345.4488 (toll free 1.800.901.3480)
Fax: 952.920.0541; email to orders@itascabooks.com

Cover Design and Typeset by Kristeen Wegner

Printed in the United States of America

Dedicated to the memory of my husband Bob Snyder and my mother Polly Ondo, who took pleasure in everyday things and found joy in the direst of circumstances.

Contents

Introduction

Tooling around the Web on one of those evenings when compulsive surfing is the only way to unwind, I bumped into a blog post about a sad-eyed beagle hanging out of its owner's arms.

"The Dog Ate My Moleskin" was the title of the post explaining how the beagle, named Sophie Lee Ramos, had eaten the 2005 Moleskin planner of her owner's former boyfriend.

The enterprising but now disoriented gent was offering on eBay, in a brown paper lunch sack, what was left of his week-old planner, in addition to "several notes, maps and diagrams from my recent holiday trip to Boston."

He commented that before its demise, when it was living safely in his back pocket, his Moleskin had served him faithfully and well and kept him on time.

I have never met Sophie Lee Ramos, and I don't own a dog. But it occurred to me, gazing at the innocent-looking beagle, that the ex-boyfriend and I have a lot in common.

We have this planner, meticulously enter our lives into it, tuck it safely away, and Shazam! Something comes along and eats it for breakfast.

The only recourse is to make the best of a life disrupted — to see the humor, laugh a little, gather up the remains in a paper bag and go on.

It was with that in mind that I decided in March 2000 to let the rest of the world know — as if there was any doubt — that my own planner was in pieces, that I did not have it all together.

Moving an elderly parent, getting kids off to camp and deciding whether to switch to a Palm Pilot were just too overwhelming when there were already Christmas stockings to stuff, Hanukkah gifts to buy, banana bread loaves to produce for the school bake sale, book groups to attend without reading the book and dancing lessons with hubby to revitalize that marriage bed spark.

That was on top of keeping track of winter gloves, trying to lose weight, collecting all the family photos in a professional-looking scrapbook, remembering to return unfortunate purchases and, during that halcyon period when the mortgage rates were low, building a house.

So instead of keeping the craziness to myself — and in hopes of restoring my own sanity — I launched "Balancing Act," a regular humor column that has appeared for nearly a decade in Suburban News Publications, a chain of 22 weekly newspapers in the Columbus, Ohio, area.

Since I launched the column, life has showered me and most Americans with even more complications. Thanks to electronic devices, our lives have speeded up. To make them simpler, we've bought even more electronic devices. We've bought fast food to keep up with the pace, but it looks like we should really be eating organics whipped up from scratch, which takes more time and money. And where do we find the hours to work more hours so we can buy this food and whip it up? If we let them, these are the quandaries that can eat at our ideal days like a pack of hungry dogs.

I've found that like the ex-boyfriend on eBay, the best way to tame the dogs that eat our planners is to find the humor in them.

Drawing on tales previously published as "Balancing Act" columns, *The Dog Ate My Planner* presents a dozen dogs, from fashion to electronic devices, from kids to elderly parents, which chomp away at the lives we've planned.

Thanks to helpful column readers and my own life experience, each dog comes with its own set of "leash laws" guaranteed to tame that pesky dog. Or make you laugh trying.

Chapter One

To "E" or Not to "E"

Quick. How much time do you spend checking your e-mail, syncing your handheld, looking up your PINs? Like Hamlet, we face a dilemma: To "E" or not to "E."

Electronic devices, those amazing time-savers, are actually a second job. If you don't believe it, try deciphering that cell phone contract — assuming your GPS actually leads you to the cell center in Columbus, Ohio, and not a pizza parlor in Kansas City.

I'm Not Ready to Hold the World in My Palm

There's a PalmPilot on my radar screen, and I'm desperate to shoot it down.

The same man who sold me on the three-inch paper planner that I cannot live without now says that a silver wizard thinner than a cigarette case is what I need to simplify my life.

"Don't you want one for Christmas?" my husband, the gadget-lover, asked months ago.

I was not sure why at the time, but I returned a very fast "No."

For a holiday moment, it staved off the tiny computer that would have allowed me to manage my schedule, keep track of my to-do list, and beam files back and forth to my lunch partner.

But the campaign resumed. And for reasons I didn't fully understand, I kept resisting — scooping up fighting words and firing them back messily as we went along.

"Cell phones are bad enough!" I told him. "This business of always being connected to somewhere else is sick. Two women can't get through a quiet lunch without Beethoven's Fifth ringing from one of their purses."

But he was persistent and clever. "Everyone is getting them," he said before beginning to recite a list of local notables, complete with their preferred models and serial numbers.

I knew it was true. I started to tell him that at work PalmPilot stories were springing up like urban legends. There was the attorney who reportedly downloaded the *Wall Street Journal* into his to read each day on the bus. And the guy who carried the entire King James Version in his Palm. But before I could get these stories out, Gadget Man was already expounding on the many available choices.

"There's the Palm IIIe, the Palm IIIx, the Palm V, the Palm Vx, the Palm VII!" he exclaimed. "You can even get them with Franklin Planner software!"

I continued to resist, still not sure exactly why, and began to suspect I might be one of those inflexible, change-hating people that corporations hire "transition consultants" to handle. With each point I made, I began to flinch at sounding more and more like my mother during the two years she resisted my dad's plea for a microwave oven.

"Why do two retired people need to bake a potato in ten minutes?" she kept asking.

"Why," I now asked, "would two people who already have three pagers, two cell phones, a fax machine and three home computers with e-mail need a second PalmPilot to simplify their lives?"

It was, of course, just the opening he needed for the final sell.

"Because the Palm is great!" he enthused. He promptly demonstrated his new one — a Palm Vx, to be exact.

"Look at this," he said. "You can carry tons of information, have addresses and phone numbers right at your fingertips, hook up to your PC, check your e-mail, beam your weekly schedule to me and carry a to-do list of 3,000 items …."

Three thousand items?

I think I just figured out why I don't want it. My mom eventually got the microwave, but there was a limit to how many potatoes she had to bake.

A Closet Palmist Comes Out

I don't know how to start this, uh, confession. But enough of holding the slender gray plastic box under the table trying to make out phone numbers in the dark. It's time I went public. I have become a closet Palmist.

Not long ago, I wrote about how my husband was campaigning to sell me on getting a PalmPilot. Gadget Man had taken the plunge and wanted to hook me on the tiny hand-held organizer/address book/calculator that was holding him hostage and organizing his life. He was relentless in this pursuit and seized upon my every weakness in an effort to persuade me. I was determined to resist.

"You could put the grocery list in it," he said, pointing out that then it would always be with me, not rumpled and helpless on the front seat of the car miles away from the produce department. I said no.

"You could enter everyone's birthday," he persisted, "and be electronically reminded every year."

But in the end, it was not a quest for perfection that did me in. It was my summer handbag. One of those mesh, woven, natural-straw affairs, it reminded me daily that I'd rather be at the beach.

Somehow, Beach Bag, slung across the shoulder of a navy business suit, invited the view that life could be lighter if I weren't toting the King James Version of Planners. Life would be better if I could simply throw one of those little gray gizmos in my bag and skip into the office. Then, I was sure, I would feel like the tall, slender, evenly tanned girls who wear the gauzy dresses in the J. Jill catalog.

I have to admit that in this respect, it worked. There is something liberating about not making a grand entrance with a book that rivals the size of Harry Potter's fourth adventure.

And at work, there is something trendy and middle-age-defying about being the first to sport a Palm. It made the Gen-Xers gawk.

"Whoa!" said co-workers young enough to be my kids. "Show us how the alarm works again. Can you really enter the same weekly meeting with one setting?"

To these fresh-faced professionals, I responded and demonstrated with unmitigated enthusiasm. I allowed them to feel how lightweight it is, to roll the tiny gray stylus in their fingers, to punch letters in the electronic keyboard and to marvel as I created to-do lists (complete with priority ratings and deadline dates), which I then sorted into neat little electronic files such as "personal" or "business" or "kids."

I omitted only a few details from my story.

I did not, for example, describe for them the morning when a low-battery warning caused me to break out in a cold sweat. I did not tell how Gadget Man skidded in to give it a "hard reset" as I wailed that my entire to-do list and birthday list and grocery list were about to vanish into cyberspace.

Nor did I share with more than a few that due to some gargantuan electronic mix-up, STRAWBERRY YOGURT — once the headliner on my grocery list — flashed for weeks as the No. 1 priority at the office.

And with no one, until now, have I shared the best part of my Palm conversion experience. This little electronic taskmaster is so small and light that some days I forget about it altogether. It simply lies sleeping with its schedules and lists and beeps all silenced somewhere in the depths of my Beach Bag.

Those are the best days of all.

Cell Bill Surprise Not a Pleasant One

I am not prepared to confess the amount. Let's just say I got a little confused last month between the 350 peak minutes and the 5,000 non-peak minutes that are included in the regular monthly fee on our cell plan.

Now, after spending enough to buy a 100-percent wool business suit (not on sale), I understand. Peak minutes are those times I can actually reach people I need to talk with but who put me on hold during the entire length of the office birthday celebration. Non-peak minutes are those hours I could probably still reach my first cousin at home in Milledgeville, Ga., but forget to call.

It all started innocently when my husband had a series of health emergencies that caused him to have four surgeries during the same cell phone period. We completely forgot we had only 15 peak minutes per weekday.

"I just called the squad," he announced on my car phone one morning at 10 o'clock." "What's up?" I asked, completely forgetting to tell him to talk fast.

He proceeded to tell me, for what is listed on the three-page printout as 4.5 minutes, every symptom that ultimately resulted in a quadruple bypass.

That launched a series of cell calls to labs and doctors' offices that are simply not open between 9 p.m. Friday and 7 a.m. Monday, when I can call anywhere in the country at no extra (35 cents a minute) charge.

The medical calls were understandable, but what followed after the shocking bill was not. First was the brief happy surprise when I called our service provider to offer a second mortgage on the house.

"Oh, my," the woman named Gloria clucked. "Shall we upgrade your plan? Just $20 for an extra 150 peak minutes a month? Let's see. You're already over a couple hundred hours for the next period. I could credit you with 500 bonus minutes."

Gratefully, I said yes. But then I discovered — with a month of unabashed cell phone use under my belt — that I was already hooked on the multi-tasker's fantasy of peak-time driving and talking and waiting on hold and driving and talking. With Gloria's extra minutes in the bank, I started ripping through peak minutes like a kid with a brand new wad of cash.

"You're always on the phone," our daughter complained as we drove along, phone planted in its little charger by the dash.

"Saves time," I explained and considered, as I called the ticket number in to the dry cleaners, whether I should also call ahead to the deli for a pound of smoked turkey.

"If the turkey's ready and waiting," I asked, "could you just run in and get it?"

"Absolutely not!" she screeched. "You need to wait in line like everybody else and take a number!"

That, I suppose, is what cell-addiction is all about. Not waiting. Not wasting a minute. And sadly, depending on the plan, paying for the extra peak minutes saved at a cost I'll never disclose.

Maybe something like Cell Phone Users Anonymous would work. "My name is Pat, and I can't stop talking until 9 p.m. on Friday."

Not everyone needs so much help, though. A friend at work says the cell phone cure is simple.

"You use them only for emergencies," she said.

I just smiled and nodded but didn't confess or ask the critical questions.

Like "How do you define emergency?" And "What if your life is just one big one?"

Free Upgrade Is Nothing to Cell-ebrate

It was inevitable. After five years with the same cell phone, I had extra batteries, a car kit that "hard-wired" it to my car, two chargers that worked, a refurbished case I bought off eBay and a weird little envelope that kept popping up to alert me to voicemail messages I didn't have.

"Oh, my," said the lady at the cell phone service center. "Look at this." She held up the square black flip phone with the little green screen to her colleagues. "Remember these?" she asked.

"Remember these?" is not a good thing to hear when you're a customer at the cell phone service center.

"The problem is your phone," she said, and proceeded to say something about people sending me text messages and pictures that I couldn't receive.

"This phone," she went on to say, "does not even have GPS tracking. If you call 9-1-1, they won't know where you are."

The thought of "they" not being able to find me in some ditch where I'd run off the road trying to retrieve a picture I thought was an emergency call put me over the edge.

"How can I fix that?" I gasped.

"How can I fix that?" is a very good thing to hear when you work at the cell phone service center, particularly when it comes with a gasp. I'm positive the entire staff looked up from their computer screens and broke out into song. "Simple!" they crooned. "We can give you a free upgrade."

Several moments of intense calculation on the other side of the counter disclosed that the free upgrade costs about the same as a free lunch. The upgrade would be free, but I'd have to buy the phone to go with it.

"Which one would you like?" she wanted to know, directing me to a wall full of smaller, shinier possibilities that have large color screens with pictures of surfers navigating huge waves on Sunset Beach.

"Something basic," I said. "I just want to make phone calls."

Basic turned out to take pictures, send pictures, choose an appropriate screensaver and identify my callers with signature rings and songs I could assign to them. Basic could even download songs off the Internet for callers whose quirks of personality or personal stories didn't quite fit the pre-programmed possibilities.

"Isn't this a little complicated?" I asked. "Assuming I ever got these rings programmed in, then I'd have to remember them."

I didn't even want to consider the possibility that someone might move or change their number or even expire, requiring their ring to be transferred with them or to someone else, or what the effect of hearing the deceased's song in an elevator somewhere might be.

"It's actually easier than the phone you have now," she said, which prompted me to launch into an elaborate public confession about how I'd never mastered the phonebook in the little black square phone.

"Don't worry," she said. "It's a three-day weekend."

By Monday morning, I'd figured out how to make the phone ring and to place a call, but I had lost my screensaver in the process. I'd added six contacts to my phone book but couldn't figure out how to assign rings to them or get them on speed dial. My success rate at answering the phone was about one in three.

"I'd help if I didn't have exams," said our daughter, who had recently programmed her own phone to play a dirge when she got a call from the house.

"I can at least fix your screensaver," she offered with a smile, planting a large picture of a martini with an olive where my "old school green screen," as she called it, used to be.

"Gee, thanks," I said. "I'm going for a walk."

For safety's sake, I threw my little GPS device in my pocket. The best that can be said is that after about a mile, trying to take a picture and send it to my husband was a nice excuse not to keep exercising.

"Was that you?" he asked when I returned.

"Great picture, huh?"

"Don't know," he said. "Just got this weird little envelope on my screen."

"You really should get a free upgrade," I told him.

Misery loves company.

Message E-ddiction
Needs a Rest

I read awhile back that the big cruise lines had started offering e-mail on some of their ships. At $5 to set up the account and another $3 to send or receive a message, cruise ship e-mail was called "the smart alternative," much cheaper than ship-to-shore calls at $6 to $11 a minute.

This is all fine. But I'm sure the real reason that e-mail hit the Love Boat has nothing to do with ship-to-shore emergencies. These cruisers had simply become e-ddicted, and the thought of five days at sea without checking their e-mail was enough to make them stay home.

Say what you want. The world is divided between people who check their messages six times a day and those who can wait a week or more. It splits between those who can let a phone ring and those who will dive over the back of a La-Z-Boy to get it.

"Let the machine get it," my husband says with a wave of his hand and keeps munching his salad. He is right, of course. Read any book about balancing your life.

But this isn't about logic. One ring of the phone, and my heart races. My mind pole-vaults to the imagined caller:

It's my mother about to pass out and gripping the phone.

"Pick up! Pick up!" she is gasping.

It's my oldest son, in Massachusetts. He has car trouble, possibly hypothermia. He is gripping his cell under a snowbank.

"I love you!" he struggles to whisper.

I leap from the table and answer.

Am I satisfied with my current phone service? Am I tired of changing light bulbs? What about refinancing the house?

Never mind the told-you-so looks. There's something redeeming about missing dinner to save the dying. I am committed to it.

But I do worry about e-ddiction. Although I've received a few e-obituaries about out-of-town relatives I barely know, I have never once received an e-mail from someone in cardiac arrest.

Mostly, just looking at the subject lines (I would never open these, of course), the e-'s I get tell how to enlarge body parts I don't have or fire my boss by working at home. Occasionally, there's something from a woman named Doris urging me to refinance the house or from someone named Ted with instructions for opening my own online casino.

Still, it's not right just letting them sit there for a whole week, unreviewed and uncared about, like my friend Lora started doing after the birth of her first child.

"Priorities," she said, looking wise for her age.

Still committed, I loyally scroll down, scouring each line hopefully for a personal nugget on the way to Delete.

"What's the point?" my husband wanted to know the other night. "It's mostly spam anyway. Give it a rest for awhile."

He is right, of course. A rest is long overdue, away from Doris and Ted and the casino business.

"Maybe we should. A complete getaway. What would you say to a cruise?"

This Robot Can Get Lost

January is a good month to stay home, not just to recover from the nonstop holiday overload but if others bought into the holiday hype like we did, nine out of 10 cars will soon be directed by robots.

"Turn right," will say the little black box that's suctioned on everyone's dash. "Exit in 800 yards."

We had hardly unwrapped our Global Positioning System before it muscled its way from under the Christmas tree onto the front seat of the car. Now the mouthy little authority is telling us how to get from unfamiliar A to never-heard-of Z without so much as a map.

"You're going to love it!" exclaimed Gadget Man, the same techno-spouse who introduced me to the PalmPilot and the seven remotes that run our TV. "It'll be great for hard-to-read street signs. When she says 'turn,' just turn. You'll never get lost again."

"But I know the way to most places I drive," I protested.

"Turn it on anyway," he said, "just for practice."

Since we seem to shop on "the European plan" (a two-minute trip to the grocery at least once day), Ms. GPS got an immediate workout, and I had to admit that on that short run, she performed flawlessly.

"Turn left," she would say. "Turn right. Turn left." And when we were smack in front of the big blue K: "You have reached your destination."

Within days, with all this success under our belts, Gadget Man insisted on programming Ms. G for the ultimate adventure: taking us to places we'd never been. Her maiden voyage into the unknown was to a hotel near our daughter's college campus in Dayton, Ohio.

"I'm OK with this," I said. "It's not like we've never been to the campus before."

"How convenient," he said. "We won't even need a map."

Our confidence built mile by mile as Ms. G instructed us to turn where we already knew we were supposed to on a trip that is essentially three freeways going either south or west.

"What if we need to make a stop?" I asked. "Can she handle that?"

"No problem," he said. "The book says she'll make the adjustment and get us back on the road. She can even figure out an alternate route if we get caught in traffic," he said. The need for a bathroom break 35 miles before the programmed exit gave her the first opportunity to strut her stuff.

"Turn around," she monotone-moaned. "Turn around and turn right."

She was only trying to help, I suppose, but her tone of voice had an attitude I didn't like.

"I feel like I'm annoying her if we stop," I told Gadget Man, "that I only get so many detours off her route."

"Don't be silly," he said. "She's a robot. She will adjust."

After the last flush, we started up again to the plea that we "Turn around."

We complied, followed her instructions to turn right and found ourselves happily back on the highway, going in the wrong direction.

"Didn't we already come this way?" I asked Gadget Man.

"Possibly," he said. "I believe you confused her when you turned around in the station to get near the restrooms."

"Pardon me," I said, horrifying Ms. G by exiting again.

"Turn around," she demanded, maliciously hoping that I would go back up the ramp to meet oncoming traffic.

"Nothing doing," I said, proceeding to enter the freeway properly, going south — an act for which she had no words.

"She must be readjusting," said Gadget Man. "She'll be back with us in a minute."

Sure enough, she was, just in time to instruct me to "Exit the highway 800 yards ahead."

This latest instruction made sense. We were clearly getting

close to the city. But there were three exits ahead, all very close together.

"Which one is 800 yards?" I asked. Before Gadget Man could answer, we were told to "Exit the highway 200 yards ahead."

"Two football fields!" he yelled, as two of the exits whizzed by. "Get off now!"

Immediately I obeyed, terrified that if I missed it, Ms. G might order me to turn around across two lanes of traffic and over the median strip. The hotel was just in view, down the road to our left.

"I told you we'd make it!" gloated Gadget Man. And, truly, she did not disappoint.

"Turn right," said Ms. G.

Help! I've Lost My Identity Through PINs

Twenty-five years ago, I had a locker at work with one of those round silver-and-black locks. Every morning, I'd zip into work and twist the dial with one hand: 14-32-2.

There was no fumbling. There were no blank stares. Just 14-32-2 and in.

I am compelled to brag about this because it is my most recent success story with anything resembling a password or PIN. Every trip to the ATM is a nightmare.

"How could you forget it again?" my husband asked again the other day when I made still another cell phone call home from the bank machine. "You use it all the time."

He knows this only because I routinely call him after trying to get cash by entering my fitness center number, my voicemail access code and my seven-digit eBay user ID.

"Just give me the PIN!" I yell, traffic lining up behind me and honking. "These people think I'm refinancing the house."

Although I am confessing to confusion, I am not owning up to complete idiocy. My first total PIN breakdown did not come until I was up to 27 different combinations of letters and numbers that were case sensitive for online shopping, an online legal research service, online bill paying with each major credit card, two online greeting card services, an online prescription service that changed every other July, and access to our internet service provider, my mother's bank card, our daughter's debit card, the swimming pool, two different consumer reporting services, six major newspapers and the members-only pages of three professional associations.

"You need a password management system," instructed my husband in one of those paternalistic moments. "You need a high-security system for storing them and getting them out."

"Not one like yours!" I said, referring to the nine-page typed list of passwords he used to store on his PC desktop until he printed it off at my request and hid it under a mattress. "Any Tom, Dick or Harry could come in and access all your personal information."

"Well, hiding Post-it Notes on the insides of file folders isn't a great system, either," he said. "I find them everywhere. And half the time, you don't even say what they go to."

"High security," I told him. "I don't even know myself."

I've considered activating one of those free software programs that promises to manage passwords for you. But I'm afraid that after I enter the passwords and my bank account numbers and e-mail addresses, I will be financing a red SUV for a 19-year-old in Nevada.

Still, in my own way, I continue to try. Occasionally, like a middle schooler taking a geography test, I've written them on the palm of my hand. Once, I hid one as a phone number in my PalmPilot. Unfortunately, I didn't remember it was there until three months had passed and I was still getting busy signals from my first cousin in Milledgeville, Ga.

I've read that biometrics may be the answer. Rather than remembering passwords or PINs, we can have our irises and retinas scanned, our fingerprints digitized and our voices recognized.

Apparently, "$200 in 20s, please," stated in my own true voice, might cause the ATM to spit out 10 crisp, green bills from my own account or, if I have a cold, from somebody else's.

"We're not there yet," my husband cautions me. "Until we are, you really need a password management system. And while you're at it, you should lock your cell phone so no one else can call from it."

He's not fooling me with that one. Sometimes I have to pay cash.

Digitals Aren't a Pretty Picture

Awhile back, I discovered that the best way to relieve midday stress was not to go to the gym or to meditate. It was to sneak out of the office at lunchtime and shoot pictures of trees.

My camera didn't have a 3x Optical Zoom lens, or any zoom lens. It didn't have three noise reduction features. And it didn't, so far as I know, have Conversion Lens Compatibility with VAD-PEA.

But it was easy and cheap and disposable, and most trees are photogenic.

"Wow!" my friends would say when I sent them a greeting card with a shot of some sprawling, leafless sculpture glued on it. "If you took that with a disposable camera, just imagine what you could do with a digital!"

Unfortunately, I did start imagining that and then obsessing over it and then — like a patient just diagnosed with a rare disease — started Googling my way to an instant education about digital photography. I could not learn enough about the available pixels and zooms and reductions as I surfed in search of the perfect camera.

"Any beginner should have no trouble coming to grips with this digital," one site bragged. I skipped over the apology that it was a simple model without a "histogram feature or custom white-balance setting" and rushed happily to the words "simplicity is a blessing."

Besides the can-do hype, the write-up presented overwhelming evidence that this camera was for me. With little effort, it had taken giant pictures of fern fronds that Ansel Adams would have loved. I could even see the little spores on their backsides. And besides the ferns, it had taken a full-face portrait of a chocolate lab and then one of his eye, big as a marble. Besides those, it had captured a bee feasting on a rhododendron and then that same bee, magnified to the size of the Goodyear blimp, sucking on flower stamens that were waving as impressively as an entire field of wheat. I raved. I gawked. I came the closest I ever have to e-dating.

"I've got to have it!!!" I told my family, and I went on about all the previously unexamined tree parts that would soon be mine.

A trip to a local discount store sealed our fatal attraction. Within a day, I was unpacking a 6" x 6" box claiming to contain a "smart zoom," 5.0 megapixels, a USB terminal and something called MPEG Movie VX.

Unfortunately, it also came with a 112-page instruction book printed in six-point type. "No time to read this now," I told my husband. "Tonight, I'll just figure out how to charge the batteries. And then tomorrow, I will probably amaze you."

He threw me a knowing look, possibly because I've never tackled the instructions to our toaster oven.

The first day went fine. I located the memory stick, put it in, zoomed in and out, and snapped dozens of pictures of trees. Sad to say, like fish that got away, they were large and beautiful but failed to get "memorized" onto the stick.

"Of course they didn't," our daughter said. "You didn't press this and this." She flashed her fingers over some buttons.

"Where does it say to do that?" I asked, pointing to the book.

"Here," she said, pointing to a mark on the camera that was as tiny as the "amen" at the end of the Lord's Prayer when it's etched on the head of a pin. "It's easy."

"Not for me," I said, groping for the book. For the next couple weeks, I worked on "setting the date and time," a regimen that comes a good 10 pages before "basic still image shooting — using auto mode." But I figured I could get there by Christmas if I didn't stop to bathe or do dishes and laundry.

Of course, before then come autumn leaves and trick-or-treaters and Thanksgiving turkeys — all of which beg to be photographed. So I've stocked up on a few more disposables just to tide me over til Christmas or possibly next summer or until I move into a retirement home.

It's not that I'm slow or techno-freaked. I just believe, like all the great photographers, that "simplicity is a blessing."

TV Skills Are Remote

I don't watch much TV. I'd like to say this is because reality TV isn't deep enough for me. Or *Friends* is too predictable. Or John McLaughlin offends me.

But none of those high-minded reasons apply. The real truth is, I can't work the remote.

Remotes, that is. We're now up to seven lined up in military order on the coffee table. I think there are a couple more under the couch cushion. They are all essential, my husband says, to the efficient running of the contents of our otherwise unimpressive "entertainment center." Each one, it seems, works a different machine.

Every few months, we've had an orientation session. But recently, when several unexpected surgeries laid him up and made him a TV slave for weeks, Gadget Man had time to begin more serious remote control training. Starting, as usual, with the one marked "TV."

"This one is just basic," he explains once again, but now with pain-killer-induced patience. "All it does is turn on the TV and control the volume." He hands over a sleek gray plastic control. It has 36 buttons, I notice. How basic is that?

"It changes channels, too," I say.

"Nooooo!" he screeches, diving across the couch. (We're near the three-hour point on pain-killer). "Never change channels on this one. It always stays on 3. You use the cable remote to change channels."

Without knowing it, he has summed up the problem. Every single remote claims to do every possible thing. The TV remote has all sorts of buttons that say they run a VCR and a DVD and something called a "theater," as well as a V-Chip, a sleep timer and something called a "Hyper Sur."

I point this out, and Gadget Man squints.

"OK," he says. "There is a button to push on here if you want to watch DVDs, even though we also have a DVD remote, which I'm getting to in a minute."

I reach for the little button under the red letters "DVD."

"No!!!" he screeches again. (We're near the four-hour point on the pain-killer). "Never change it to 'DVD.' Just go to the little button under 'Video 1.' It's marked 'input'. And you can use it for the karaoke machine, too."

With that piece of news, we move on to the cable remote, which has at least as many buttons for changing cable channels, which is allowed, but the thing to remember here is that you never push the number of the channel you want.

"Hit cable 7 for channel 34," he says. "Look it up on the back of the TV guide. There's a little chart."

The cable box remote is not to be confused with the VCR remote, which he explains is capable — if I hit No. 5 — of programming the VCR to pick up certain shows during the day or night automatically.

"Don't push 5!" he warns. "You stick with Play and Stop. And don't even go near express programming."

The order is possibly easy to follow since this remote, like the one for the TV, doesn't label any button to say what it actually does. Nothing says "express programming." I'm dying to push the 5 button but am scared something terrible will happen. Maybe the gazebo will blow up in the neighbor's backyard. I sit on my hands.

Finally, we go over the DVD remote, the newest in our electronic family. I like it. The power button is red. Oddly, it says "power." Apparently pushing this red button will power up the DVD as long as the blue power button on the TV remote is on and the "input" button has been activated.

A few run-throughs and I'm pointing and clicking and remembering which channel is for the cable and whirring around DVDs. I remember this for about as long as I used to remember after a science test that PSBEWV stood for all the parts of a simple leaf.

"How about labeling them?" I ask, handing over a roll of masking tape and a ballpoint pen. "Just say what it works and what to push."

Gadget Man rolls his eyes but begins to dictate VCR directions with the urgency of a dowager on her death bed bequeathing the family silver: "Press Power," "Put Tape In," "Fast Forward Past Preview," "Press Play."

Labels on every control, I am in business until one of our daughter's high-tech friends turns one over and giggles.

"Oh, my gosh!" she says. "You've got to be kidding!"

Mysteriously, the labels vanish. Bits of adhesive say "Press" or "Play" but never what.

No matter, I tell her. Who has time for TV? I'm much too busy with Shakespeare.

Leash Laws

PDAs. Paper or plastic? Anyone who thinks this question just comes up at the grocery store has never been to a store that sells planners. There's the clunky paper planner or the tiny PDA. Which to choose? If the dog eats your paper planner, it's gone, at least in its original form. If the dog eats your PDA, the dog may be burping and chiming every 15 minutes, but hopefully you have a back-up copy on your PC. So if you can have only one, I say get a PDA. If you can afford both, I say indulge. I realize this is contrary to time management gurus who say to avoid two calendars like the plague. But I see nothing wrong with us paper-and-pen types keeping some sort of paper book for planning purposes as long as the PDA is always current.

Cell phones. Contrary to popular belief, it's possible to read a cell phone contract and have your questions ready before you join that sweaty Saturday afternoon crowd at the cell phone store. The Consumers Union, the nonprofit organization that publishes *Consumer Reports*, provides free help online that explains how the contracts work and even directs consumers to major provider contracts to download and read before visiting the store. Here's the link: http://www.consumersunion.org/pub/core_telecom_and_ utilities/000732.html.

E-mail. Hold on a minute. I have to check my e-mail . It's OK because it's 11 a.m. — which, along with 4 p.m., is an acceptable time to check e-mail according to Timothy Ferriss in his time management blockbuster *The 4-Hour Workweek*. The idea is that by limiting when e-mail can intrude, we take control of our lives. Anyone concerned about missing a critical, time-sensitive message can leave an auto message: For example, "I only check e-mail at noon and 4 p.m. If this matter needs attention before then, you may call my cell phone (insert number)." (By the way, my only messages, when I just checked, were from online catalogs selling travel wear).

GPS. Use it if you must. But just in case … check several online mapping services such as Mapquest, Google Maps, and Yahoo Maps. Pick the directions that make the most sense (i.e., do not have a succession of quarter-mile U-turns), and make yourself a Dummy's guide, that is, a manila file folder for the passenger seat that has the major moves listed in bold Sharpie marker and the online directions and map stuffed inside. Just in case.

PINs. I used to keep my contacts in a Rolodex and my PINs in my head. That was when I had only two PINs. Now I keep my contacts in Microsoft Office and my PINs in the Rolodex. Every time I create a new, magic user ID or password, it goes on a Rolodex card and is handy when I need it. Of course, the highly sensitive ones, like the routing number for my Swiss bank account, stay in my head or on a Post-it Note on the bottom of a clay pot in the far corner of the basement. Don't tell.

Digital cameras. Get a second job if you must, but if you are techno-challenged or have trouble with fine print, buy your camera from a camera store that has friendly photographers behind the counter and offers classes and ongoing help. When Ansel Adams got into trouble, he didn't seek out a sales clerk who usually sold garden supplies.

Remotes. Two weeks before your birthday, purchase a lovely loose-leaf notebook and present it to the king, queen, prince or princess of your local remote with the following message inside: In lieu of _____ (flowers, dinner out, a new tie or a new car), please create illustrated instructions for each of our ___ (4, 6, 8) remotes, place them in this book and wrap it up for me along with an agreement to conduct a live demonstration and update instructions in the event of equipment changes.

Chapter Two

If It Weren't for Kids and Dogs....

"Children! Without them, what would we do for worries?" I've never stopped asking that age-old question. Kids worry us, weary us, inspire us. On so many days, it is the children — not the dog — who eat the planner down to the very last second.

Parents Search for Lazy Days of Summer

The school bus is just around the bend. And the greatest joy, as the yellow giant squeaks to a halt, will be that it comes at the same time each day and that someone else is driving.

This is especially true for the more ambitious parents among us. By August, they have already driven enough miles around town to go to Arizona.

Lured by lesson and activity descriptions that outdo a college catalog, these amazing troopers have shunned the easy road — same old day camp or babysitter every day — and sprung instead to enrich their children's lives with a custom-made summer.

I am in awe of the logistics that I am beyond handling. Swimming lessons here. Adventure camp there. Carpooling everywhere.

It was heartening to hear the other day that this poses a challenge for even the super-organized.

In a moment of frustration, my friend Deb confided, "The problem is, nothing lasts for over a week! There has been no one routine. I have to check my calendar for everything because I can't remember from one week to the next which camp is going on, which day is my day to carpool! I'm melting …"

Anyone who thinks a simple calendar will do has only a passing, second-hand acquaintance with the concept of childhood enrichment. With so much going on, there's no time to look at a calendar.

Case in point is our cousin Karen, who recently managed to compose a frustrated, six-page e-mail on the topic of enrichment. This was between completing medical forms and ordering T-shirts for her middle son to play soccer, basketball and tennis on alternate weeks and her oldest to attend "history day camp (a different day, a different field trip)" and go on a llama expedition while the two-year-old stayed home with the 10th nanny of the year. All, she said, because other kids in the neighborhood were away at vacation or camp, and there was no one left at home to play with.

E-mail was handy. She was already on the word processor trying to recoup fees for the week she'd mistakenly signed each boy up for two camps at once.

But considering she had two in school to enrich, her activity numbers were hardly more impressive than those of my girlfriend Darryl, who with viola lessons, music camp, lacrosse camp and soccer camp, was enriching only one.

Darryl, though, managed to sound less harried and more philosophical.

"It could be so much worse if we also had homework to do every night and projects on the weekend," she said.

The good news is that there may be relief on the way. I'm told by one veteran that the secret to keeping it all straight is a spiral notebook, started just about now — with a page for each child for each week of the next summer. Then, as the brochures begin to roll in and the camp fairs begin, the pages get filled with due dates for early-bird deposits and medical forms. No more double payments.

For super-enrichment achievers, I suppose there could be a Summer Enrichment Planner with pocket dividers for every week, customized to hold information on dozens of early-bird deposits and medical forms, all theoretically transferable into a beeping electronic organizer for a never-miss summer.

But who am I to say? On July 15, my organizer beeped to tell me that it was the first day of school.

I wouldn't trust it to tell me when to send our daughter off with a llama.

Can You Bake?
The Answer Is Easy

Is it the back-to-school ads, or the occasional nip in the air? I don't know. But at this time of year, I'm vulnerable. You name it, and I want to sign up.

Just about anything will do: massage classes, workshops on making door decorations from eucalyptus leaves, all-you-can-eat classes on cooking with saffron.

So it's especially bad timing that just about now, those rainbow stacks of school forms have come home again.

"Volunteer Sign-Up!" These laundry lists of spare time possibilities slide out of a backpack and into my waiting fingers as easily as an atomic tangerine Crayola. And when they do, I shout "Hallelujah" and run for a pencil.

Business hours save me from myself during school hours. It's tough to be at work and also teaching English as a second language at 10 a.m. on alternate Thursdays. But baking? Absolutely!

Without a moment's thought, I have always responded with a vibrant "Yes!" — to the fall bake sale, the class Halloween party, the November band concert, the holiday cookie swap, the President's Day snack, the Valentine's celebration, the winter bake sale, the carnival cakewalk, the Spring Fling dance, the teacher appreciation luncheon, the spring bake sale and the end-of-school picnic.

I have survived these bursts of enthusiasm only because I have learned the secret. When the forms ask, "Can you bake?" it means the school is simply curious. Getting close to an oven is strictly optional.

It took me awhile to understand this. In the early days, when the children and I were much younger, if I'd signed up for two dozen iced Valentine cookies, I was hauling out the flour and a grease-soaked recipe card at midnight. If I agreed to bring cupcakes, I was scouring old magazines to find instructions for the ones that look like ice cream cones with sprinkles.

Now, I know that answering "yes" simply means, "Yes, I have baked in my life, and I know the art of presentation." This is very important.

For instance, it would never occur to a person who has never baked brownies that the proper way to present the ones from the Wonder Bread Thrift Store is to snip them out of the individual plastic wrappers, sprinkle them with powdered sugar and place them on a doily.

A person who has never baked banana bread might never imagine that the way to donate a loaf is to remove it carefully from the Entenmann's box, sprinkle it with powdered sugar and wrap it in Saran Wrap.

Of course, by fifth grade, most do understand that a sack of Chips Ahoy travels nicely in a backpack. If not needed for Halloween, it can be stashed in the supply cabinet and used as "behavioral incentives" on Friday afternoons near the end of school, when each child who does not burp loudly after lunch receives two.

None of this is to say that baking is not a way to relax or get life back in balance. There can be something calming about making sugar cookie dough, and chilling it, and rolling it, and cutting it, and baking it, and cooling it and icing it. And I fully intend to do it whenever I have time — at least once every 10 years.

De-Stress with a Sigh of Relief

"You are sooo calm," my friend Beth said the other day. "If my 16-year-old daughter had called to say she was taking the train into New York City with a friend, I'd have been a basket case."

"At least it was a short ride from her friend's house in Jersey," I said. " At least she wasn't calling from a tattoo parlor. At least she wasn't stranded under 17 tons of terrorist rubble on the subway."

Beth's eyes grew wider.

"Who would think such things?" she asked.

"Only," I confessed, "a world-class catastrophizer."

It's true. While others might imagine an ordinary traffic jam on the way to work, I am capable of more. An entire bridge might collapse under the rush hour weight. A tanker might explode.

"The beauty of envisioning disaster," I explained, "is that after imaging the worst, an ordinary crisis is welcome relief. Imagine how relaxing it is to know I'm 45 minutes late to work because of a stalled car."

Beth seemed unconvinced that catastrophizing will one day replace yoga, but I think there is no doubt.

It requires absolutely no equipment and can be done in the middle of anything else. In a word, it is the complete stress reliever for multi-taskers.

"Sorry," she said. "I don't see how worrying can help."

Right away, I knew she was no good at catastrophizing. Anyone who puts worrying and catastrophizing in the same league has never elevated the C-word to an art form.

A worrier, facing company for dinner, might fret over the menu or where to seat people.

A catastrophizer takes it to a whole new level. First, there is the possibility of food poisoning, which will not manifest itself until the guests are back home, or worse, an allergic reaction, which requires the immediate arrival of paramedics at the dinner hour, always a curiosity for the neighbors. Ultimately, there is the prospect of a lawsuit, in which one will argue futilely that the garnish really did look like nasturtiums and murder was not intended.

Only a world-class catastrophizer, not a mere worrier, experiences the enormous relief of the after-dinner phone call from a still-healthy guest requesting the recipe.

I was inspired to catastrophize by my father, who believed that "only 90 percent of the things we worry about come to pass." He added cheerily that it was the other 10 percent, coming out of nowhere, that usually did us in. It did not take long to figure out that if 90 percent of the things we worry about do not happen, then at least 95 percent of the things we catastrophize about will never happen. That leaves me vulnerable only five percent of the time.

Of course, the best opportunities for catastrophic stress relief come from raising children and teen-agers, who could be destined either to be hit by cars after failing to look both ways or to hit others with them driving 95 mph while drinking a beer from the family refrigerator.

Worriers wait up for their offspring but fall asleep before curfew. Catastrophizers stay awake and remember the movies they watched in drivers ed class 25 years ago. Assuming junior arrives home safely, catastrophizers are still up to appreciate the sigh of relief they are breathing.

Although I explained all this to Beth, she still was not convinced.

"It's better to breathe deep with yoga than with relief," she said.

Maybe she's right. If I were not a catastrophizer, I would not have sent our young traveler emergency cash and instructed her to call from NYC every seven minutes on her cell. And I would not have received the most disturbing message of all.

"Hi, Mom! Guess where we are: Tiffany's. And we just left Henri Bendel."

My dad was right. It's what comes out of nowhere that gets you in the end.

Track's Hard to Fit into Fast-Track Life

With three kids, I've been through the worlds of baseball and football and soccer.

But none of those action-packed sports prepared me for the sport of choice this spring. I just wasn't ready for track.

Sure. There was the lengthy sheet called "Cautions, Considerations, and Responsibilities to Increase Safety and Enjoyment of Interscholastic Track and Field" that my 13-year-old daughter and I signed. She was instructed always to "follow a hard day with an easy day," to drink eight glasses of water, to take a day off each week.

There were written instructions about shoes and diet and leg pain and how to behave in the locker room. And there was the most organized list of events and start times that I've ever seen, complete with directions to every field.

But one tiny detail was missing from the schedule: the end time for each meet. This was perhaps not so much an effort to mislead as an astonishing show of honesty. The truth is, track meets do not end. And if they do, it's just in time for a bedtime snack.

This is except for the ones that launch the season, when the chill factor is 18 degrees. Those take an hour longer than the rest. At least that was what Track Dad told me as we were pinned one April evening, backs flat against a brick concession stand in Hilliard, Ohio, trying to suck in the warmth of a once-sunny day.

"Can't move," he said, teeth chattering. "Might miss her."

This is the truth. Never in the history of school track has a single runner ever been scheduled to run events back to back. One's at 5 … one's at 6:30 … one's at 8. Or thereabouts. And each

33

time, for only about four minutes. So anyone who leaves to sit in the car or to get another kid at another sporting event may miss the moment.

After the first few meets, it quickly occurred to us that despite its name, track is not a sport that fits easily into a fast-track life.

The multi-taskers among us brought briefcases and flapped around after wayward business papers. We made cell phone calls above "Last call for the Girls' 200." We fidgeted. We read the paper.

We began to make business plans. What if we rented pagers that flashed and vibrated? "Stay warm in the comfort of your car. We'll page you when your kid is up."

What if we sold gold cards? "For a $200 donation, your kid will run in the first event, first heat. For $150, first event, second heat ...."

What if we started music lessons? "Can't fit clarinet in during track season? Come on out to our van, 7:30, right after the boys' high jumps."

They were all wonderful entrepreneurial fantasies, and although it seemed impossible at the time, the season was too short to launch a single one.

But that, I'm surprised to say, is not my only regret.

Now that it's over, I sort of long for those long, quiet evenings. Toward the end, I don't know if it was wisdom or resignation, but we seemed to be better at waiting. We were starting to hang out like a bleacher full of fishermen, just sitting there, breathing evenly, waiting for a bite.

Maybe I'm romanticizing, but who knows? When we finally learned how to slow down and wait, maybe we, too, were becoming long-distance runners. Even without the track shoes.

Helicopter Parent? Who? Me?

As a mother of three, I've always been slightly behind. I had never heard of the Home Shopping Network till my younger son reported that his friend Jake's mother watched it daily. She made the best nachos el grande, too. (El what?)

I never knew pugs wore tuxedos to pug parties till my oldest and his wife sent me pictures of our granddog at one. (Tuxedos?)

But I had to drop the youngest at college last month to learn the latest. My husband and I may look like parents, but we are actually helicopters.

The news came in an address by the dean of students. "Many of you are up there hovering," he explained, "ready to swoop down at a moment's notice to save your student before they try to solve their problems themselves."

Like pug parties and TV shopping, I don't know how I missed this. A Google search revealed that campuses around the country are hiring staff just to deal with us baby boomer helicopters.

"Cell phones," said one report, "have become the longest umbilical cord in the world." It went on to tell about parents who e-mailed their children daily, registered their students for classes, chose their majors, argued with their professors about their grades and later attended their job interviews and negotiated their salaries.

"These have been the most protected and programmed children ever," the report said, quoting one university dean who mentioned car seats, safety helmets, play groups, soccer leagues, cell phones and e-mail, for a score of 100 percent at our house.

"Do you think we're really like that?" I asked my husband, who had sent a letter a day to our daughter at summer camp.

"Absolutely not," he said.

At times like this, when my parenting has been questioned, I reach for evidence of model behavior, no matter how relevant.

"I never let the boys eat sugary cereal," I said. "And I

stopped doing her laundry around fourth grade. She told me her friends' parents still did it, so that would not be hovering."

My husband joined in. "This summer, when she said we had nothing to eat, I told her, 'Go buy groceries yourself.' And I just e-mailed her that she'd be fine on her own."

"Her computer isn't even set up yet."

"I wanted to be the first," he said.

"It's really her brothers who are the helicopters," I told him. "They called her twice during the senior prom."

"Brothers," he said. "They're so overprotective."

I failed to mention that I was still carrying around her class schedule in my purse so I'd know where she was during the day, that my cell phone was in my pocket so I didn't miss any calls, and although her brothers' speed dials eluded me, I knew hers was 3.

But I knew better than to call her. I'd checked out an online survey ("How do you know if you're a helicopter parent?") and I wanted badly to pass. There were four categories. The first was "You are in constant contact with your child." Constant contact was defined as calling at least once a day or getting a call from a child "at any sign of stress or trouble."

"I have not called her once," I announced to my husband 18 hours after leaving her, "and she has not called me."

I was also relieved to note that I had not crossed the line in any of the other three categories. I had not been in constant contact with school officials, decided on my child's major, researched a paper for her or felt bad if she failed a course. Never mind that classes had not yet started.

"No one can really know if you're a helicopter except your child," her father opined.

As usual, he made lots of sense.

"Let's call her and ask," I said.

They're Only a Phone Call Away

Many years ago, my now-grown boys gave me a little stained glass plaque. Around the milk-white calla lilies wound the wisdom: "You never outgrow your need for mom."

At the time they were 5 and 9, and I was touched by their insight. Apparently, I'd done so well answering their slightly disturbing questions ("Have you seen my Popsicle?") that as adults they would not be able to do without me.

Only then, we would not have the constant interruptions, the constant running for clothes and school supplies and soccer. The need for mom would instead be for wisdom, for high-level conversation and for answers to life's more ponderous questions.

"Can you take a moment to review my business plan?" they would ask. Or "How can we achieve world peace?"

So when the sensitive, deep-thinking oldest moved out of state and married, I could hardly wait for the calls.

"How's life?" I wanted to know.

"OK," he said. "But I'm filling out this form. When did I have a tetanus booster?"

"That's all you want to know?"

"Actually, no," he said. "I need our address in 1982."

Since then, he has called three times to see if I have a certified copy of his birth certificate (I don't) and twice for the county where he was born so he could send off for one with the address I gave him a couple times before but he lost it.

"Do you remember who my doctor was when I had knee surgery in high school?" he wanted to know the other night.

"Why?" I asked.

"I think I messed up my cartilage," he said. "If you possibly still have his phone number ...."

I used to think that parents who maintained the most contact with their adult children owned condos in Florida and family cottages by lakes. Now I understand that they simply have good filing systems.

"Hold on," I told the one with the bad cartilage. "I've got his name and address here somewhere. " And before long, I had not only the doctor's phone number but the original post-surgical instructions in case of nausea.

This is my downfall. I have become so indispensable at nailing life's trivia that someone else is apparently left to provide him with career advice and debate an exit strategy for Iraq. While he turns to others for leisurely, philosophical conversations, I am left to recite his grandma's home phone number on a dime (she's had the same one for six years) and remind him that it's his sister's birthday.

It's almost the same with the younger one, who lives in town. He's called a few times looking for his wallet, his keys and his cell phone but normally checks in with more worrisome questions: "What if my dog swallowed a whole bottle of Advil?" and "Have you ever been to the impound lot?"

In my garage are a couple of kites he wants left out in case the wind is good. In the basement are some Pinewood Derby cars. In my PalmPilot are the name of his doctor and the best directions for getting there from his last three addresses.

"Haven't these guys ever discovered MapQuest or Google?" my husband wanted to know the other night after the phone rang twice during a sit-down dinner.

I tried to sigh impressively and roll my eyes.

"It's useless," I whined. "If I wrote it all out, they'd just lose it. I'm destined to be interrupted forever."

At least, I hope.

Long-Distance Granddog
Is a Handful

An expert at simplifying my life, I am not. Just ask my husband. If we're ahead of schedule for a doctor's appointment, I see no point in taking a book and waiting.

"Let's see if the 10-minute oil change really is," I'll say, pulling into the nearest Jiffy Lube.

And so it is with great regret that I have never been able to complicate our lives by buying a pet. If it weren't for my spouse's allergies, I'd haul home an English sheepdog in a minute.

"What about shots?" I've asked, "or acupressure treatments?" Sneezing at the thought, he will not relent. It's only through the kind-heartedness of my oldest son and his wife that I am experiencing the joys of complicating my life with dog ownership.

"You will soon have a granddog," they called one fall from Massachusetts to announce.

The great or unfortunate news, depending on your point of view, was that The GDog , a pug puppy, would be living out of state.

"Perfect!" said my husband.

"Too far away!" said I.

Thanks to the wonders of digital photography, though, we have been able to share the dilemmas, without the dander, of raising Winston Tate.

Two months in, I can say that the granddogging experience can be compared only to the time I brought his owner home from the maternity ward.

"It will change your life forever," said my mother at the time, in what I wanted to believe was a lilting tone of voice.

"Children!" said a friend with several. "Without them,

what would you do for worries?"

I know now that you would get a dog.

First, there was the issue of training the GDog.

"We've decided on crate training," announced my son in a call around Thanksgiving. He proceeded to describe how the GDog would somehow be confined in a crate for short periods while they were home, to learn bladder control.

"And when you're both at work?" I gasped.

"My boss is letting me bring him to work for the first five weeks," he said.

The next call, substantially less than five weeks later, reported that the GDog was now in doggie day care.

"Winston is very vocal," he said, without elaboration. "Besides, this will help him develop social skills."

Wanting to be a model grandma, I kept my concerns about germs to myself and simply applauded the parents' good judgment in purchasing doggie health insurance before any pre-existing conditions developed.

The e-mail traffic that followed from the GDog's parents suggested ongoing debate over the amount of socialization required at such a tender age, the value of having canine vs. human playmates and the importance of delayed gratification in raising a mature, responsible pug. In his most recent photo, the GD is sporting a pacifier.

"What do you think?" I asked my husband the other day. "Is he too young for doggie day care? Is the pacifier OK?"

"Not your problem," he said.

Of course, he's right. But still, I booked a flight to Massachusetts.

Not that I would interfere. But life is short, and I needed to tour Emily Dickinson's home.

Leash Laws

Summer enrichment. A friend of mine, a single mom with limited resources, kept it simple when her daughter was small by enrolling her in summer daycare (no choice; she had to work) and reserving a small cabin by a lake for a week or two at the end of the summer. There they went, the two of them, with some board games, fishing poles and library books. When her daughter was older, they crammed in a week of band camp and honors camp but always returned to the lake at the end of the summer. They didn't seem to need any special planning tools, and as far as I know, they never double-booked. Try it.

Baking. When I wrote about baking, several readers asked what doilies are. Several more asked where to find them. The doilies that go under the store-bought goodies that clever women take to bake sales are paper doilies, and grocery stores like to display them in unlikely areas, sometimes hanging from clips in the Chinese food section, sometimes by the dog food. As soon as there's a doily sighting, the trick is to grab a large quantity in several sizes. That way, no midnight runs to the mini-mart, which doesn't carry them anyway.

Catastrophizing. I must confess that my theory of catastrophizing for inner peace has been debunked by best-selling author Eckhart Tolle, who points out in *The Power of Now* that greater peace comes from being in the moment. Or, to summarize his 224 pages: "When you're there, be there." So instead of saying "Oh my God, oh my God," say "When you're there, be there," and you'll be both peaceful and trendy.

Sports. First, try the be-there mantra. Then, when you discover that no one can be there for a five-hour track meet, just try to be there and not off getting a hot dog when junior leaves the starting gate or hits a homer. Best way: Sit next to over-eager parents of a teammate running the same event. They will always know who's up to bat or to run. They will even have a copy of the track schedule, which, miraculously, they will know how to read.

Helicopter parent. Putt-putt-putt-putt-putt. If you're inclined to be too involved in your college student's life, tell your friends and ask them to make like a helicopter every time they see you swooping down. "I disagree!" you will say, explaining why this time you must get involved. "Au contraire!" they will say. And on and on. By senior year, you will have properly disengaged. Or alienated your children and all your friends.

Long-distance children. OK, so the children rarely call for mountain-moving advice, only for the name of their kindergarten teacher or instructions on boiling eggs. It is not that you are an inadequate mentor, only that you are a niche parent. Your niche? The minutiae of their lives. Heck, life coaches can be hired and fired. Only you know when they got their tetanus shots.

Congratulations, you're not expendable.

Long-distance pets. Use same vocabulary as for long-distance grandchildren: *Wow! He's brilliant! Trust your own good judgment.* As opposed to: *But don't you think ....If I were you .... Not to worry you, but ....* I'm no scientist, but I'm thinking there's a correlation between grandparent vocabulary and frequency of invitations. Just guessing.

Chapter Three

Fashion and Other Time Wasters

Whether it's sorting through shoes, keeping tabs on winter gloves, staying wrinkle-free and immaculately manicured, or obsessively accessorizing over eBay, fashion is inevitably one of those dogs that eats your planner.

Long Fingernails?
Give Me a Break

Until last month, I was just vaguely curious about the fingernail parlors popping up everywhere — the ones that feature long, curving nails once reserved for the likes of Howard Hughes.

Why, I wondered, would any woman want to glue on acrylic nails half as long as her fingers? Why would anyone want to paint birds on her tips?

But two weeks before my younger son's wedding, I became a believer.

"Don't be a frump," said my friend Beth. "Don't go looking like a mother of the groom."

She had a point. At every wedding I remember, there's the bride's mom: Ivory soap twin of the bride, dabbing her waterproof mascara with a tissue, glowing. And there's the mother of the groom: short hair, good perm, wire glasses.

The "broom" knows the intimate details of the veil, the number of Jordan almonds in the little tulle bags at the reception table and the name of every person seated at Table 17.

The "moom" simply hopes that the groom climbs out of the fishing boat in time for the ceremony and has enlisted a friend — just in case — to drive the getaway car.

"The least you can do," counseled Beth, clasping my hands, "is to have good fingernails." She looked again. "The least you can do is to *have* fingernails."

Within days, I located a nail artiste who presided over a little studio that smelled like a body shop for scratch-and-dent work.

"How long will this take?" I checked, as she lined up little bottles of magical potions and polish beside a full set of long, white Cruella De Vil tips.

"Oh, not long," she droned, offering the first in a series of little fibs on the subject of how long anything would take while wearing acrylic nails.

"Just relax and enjoy."

An hour or so later, after being accused several times of being "the restless type" and instructed to plant all 10 tips quietly under a nail dryer that looked suspiciously radioactive, I emerged.

Just two days before the wedding and 30 minutes after debating the merits of Venus di Violet and Not So Bora-Bora-ing Pink, I had gained a full deck of "stylishly conservative" nails (shorter, no birds) and the inability to open a can of pop without a screwdriver.

"They look fabulous!" my husband exclaimed.

"You drive," I replied. "I can't dig for my keys."

Over the next two days, I discovered that the glamour of artful nails has nothing to do with glamour. Their beauty is that they are totally disabling.

"Could you type this paper for me?"

"Not with these nails."

"Light bulb in the bathroom needs changing."

"Sorry. Can't turn the screws."

"Dinner ready?"

" As soon as you open the box."

For a couple of days, it looked like a $30 nail job could bring not only glamour to the "moom" but as much relaxation as a full-body massage.

But sad to say, the nails in the end were not as picture-perfect as the wedding.

The honeymoon was over on the morning after when a quarter-inch chip of Venus di Violet landed on the kitchen counter during an ill-advised attempt to open a quart of milk. Then there was the file drawer at work and the begonia pot that the groom's grandma noticed needed drain holes.

Finally, thanks to a giant toenail clipper, leisurely soaks in acetone and hours of picking and peeling with the zeal of a child removing school glue, the rest disappeared without a trace. But not without a lesson learned.

I hear that extending the family can bring a pleasant new layer of chaos to an already overbooked life. But now if I need a break, I know just where to go.

The only question is the color: Pistol Packin' Pink or Wyatt Earple Purple?

Crisp Clothes:
A wrinkle in Time Management

I'd like to say I'm planning a trip around the world. I'd like to say I'm suiting up for a safari or a jaunt between London and Paris on the Eurostar.

But the real reason I'm shopping for travel clothes has nothing to do with travel. The skirts and shirts that can be folded to the size of a washcloth without wrinkling are the only ones I have time to take care of.

A trip through the mounting pile of spring clothing catalogs proves my point.

"The look of linen!" proclaims one page. "The natural feel of cotton!" exclaims another.

This would all be as fine as the cool and collected women in the pictures if they were not actually wearing linen and cotton. But alas, they are wearing linen and cotton. And sadly, despite the claims that a rumpled "hassle-free" version is fashionable, they seem to be wearing them ironed.

"Don't ever buy linen," my mother warned me years ago as she slipped an otherwise perfectly good dress into an AmVets box. "You can spend all night ironing it, and the minute you sit down, you've got a big crease across the front."

This truth explains why the women in the catalogs are never pictured sitting down but not why they are smiling so brightly. They could not be this happy. In real life, they are next to broke from the dry cleaning bills or next to exhausted from getting up half an hour early each morning to iron.

Or maybe they don't yet understand that the catalog description of what they're wearing and the care labels are two different things.

"Washable" means "Hand wash; cool iron if necessary," which in turn means "Put it in the machine, and you're looking at permanent pleats. This fabric sticks to a warm iron like raw egg to an iron skillet and must be scraped off with a dinner knife."

"Dry clean" means "$15 a pop or do-it-yourself at home" and "Touch up with a warm iron if necessary, preferably turned inside out with a damp cloth unless you'd like to see your reflection in it."

"Most people don't worry about this," my daughter insists. "They iron their clothes. They care about style. They don't limit themselves to what they can throw in a dryer."

Clearly, I am not normal. I am usually willing to limit myself to white, khaki and black. I am willing to purchase clothes with hidden pockets for passports I don't carry. And I am willing to limit myself to the one page in the non-travel catalog that claims, "Our care-free blend shirts are wrinkle-free straight from the dryer" and then bolt to the dryer at the very first buzz, which is what "straight from the dryer" really means. But I am not willing to iron.

"I just wish I could find a red tank dress that is truly wrinkle-free, or a blue one, or any dress really that is not quite so somber," I told my mom the other day.

"Easy," she said, directing me to a fabric store. "They have so many choices and so much in wash-and-wear."

The thought was momentarily appealing. But then the idea of laying out a pattern, pinning it, cutting it, and oh-my-gosh putting in a zipper kicked in.

"Actually, I like khaki," I told her. "Doesn't show the dirt, and it looks so great with a red silk scarf."

Washable silk, of course. Hand wash. Drip dry. Low iron.

Winter Adds an Extra Layer

The question seemed friendly enough, but it bit like the wind outside.

"Ma'am," asked the serious young man at the downstairs coffee bar, "did you leave your gloves here yesterday?"

He wasn't asking everyone, I noticed. Only the chief suspects. The ones who vacantly pay for their coffee, only to leave it sitting on the counter. The ones who have to commandeer an entire table for their coats and briefcases and purses while they fish for the money.

He's clearly figured out what I have long known. For the already distracted and organizationally impaired, winter adds an impossible layer.

It was hard enough a month or so ago to keep track of cell phones and pagers and security passes and electronic organizers and sunglasses and reading glasses. Now come a coat and a hat and two gloves, and on at least one day a year (it is usually lost on the first cold day of the season), a scarf.

But gloves are the worst. They pose a philosophical dilemma. Is it better to believe the best about ourselves and buy a nice, well-fitting pair to be cherished and watched as carefully as children? Or should we invest in three identical, one-size-fits-all pairs from the grocery store carousel because we know in advance that in approximately three-quarters of an hour one of them — a left or a right — will be lying abandoned on some parking lot like a crumpled candy wrapper.

This year, with an enormous collection of one-size-fits-all, right-handed, navy blue gloves in the foyer closet, I've decided it's time to focus. I've decided to spring for the good pair and try to visualize myself into a new state of "together."

In a new show of discipline, I'm going for the elegant, plain-coat look. Something svelte in camel or herringbone with tailored inset pockets, a single glove tucked discreetly in each one, right in right, left in left, both actually matching and pulled out neatly at the moment of departure.

This new image will not be easy to achieve, and given my history, I am already feeling discouraged. I suspect there's a high correlation between people who keep track of their gloves and those who always have their in-store coupons handy and know where all of their shoes are. These folks have a certain "in the moment" quality, actually focusing on the here and now instead of leapfrogging miles ahead and wondering whether getting a smallpox vaccination would kill them if they were already infected with anthrax.

But back to the original question. No, I did not leave my gloves in the coffee bar. Someone else must have walked off and left the hunter green leather beauties by the cappuccino machine.

Mine are right ... uh ... probably under the umbrella that I think I left at the orthodontist's office last week.

On eBay, Addiction Is E-Z

After years of saying I hate to shop, after once shunning a neighbor who wrapped herself in an afghan and clicked her remote all afternoon toward the Home Shopping Network, I have to confess …

I'm hooked on eBay.

Our daughter is actually to blame. She left her favorite athletic pants at summer camp. I got tired of the moaning.

"They were soooo great," she said. "Kappa pants. Black with little figures down the side. I bought them from another camper for $10. She said she bought them for $40. They don't make them anymore. I'll never replace them."

Like all of life's problems — needing more sleep, removing spots, changing wiper blades for the winter — I went straight to the Web and Googled for help.

Kappa pants, it seemed, were everywhere, but not in XS and not in black with little figures down the side. Not, that is, except for the Kappa pants that lived in the electronic auction world of eBay. There, some woman in New Haven, Conn., was hawking the very thing I needed: black XS with little figures down the side.

"Hardly worn!" proclaimed the seller, who displayed a home-shot digital photo of the Kappas lying across her living room couch. "I did cut a tiny slit on one side," she confessed, offering a zoom-in shot of the slit. It resembled the ones I've seen my daughter cut on her own pants. Not a problem. Besides, the ad carried assurances that she'd been selling on the site for a couple of years and had a 100 percent customer satisfaction rating.

"Perfecto!" I shouted, and let my husband in on the exciting find, sure to be a hit on the first night of Hanukkah.

"These are used pants?" he said. "You don't even know this person."

"Hardly worn pants," I told him. "Just like buying at a consignment shop. Besides, she was so honest about the slit. She's probably a student at Yale Divinity School."

With that, I devised an eBay password and user ID that no one else had already grabbed (the hardest part of the entire transaction) and signed myself up with some sort of payment service called PayPal that my seller preferred (the second hardest part). Then, with three days and 47 minutes remaining in the auction, I started vying for the pants against two other bidders.

"Twenty dollars and shipping," I assured my husband. "No more." And I obediently instructed eBay to keep bidding automatically for me, but only up to $20.

Such revelry followed when the Kappas appeared on the first night of Hanukkah that by Christmas, eBay alerted me that I'd earned five feedback comments and was halfway to a yellow star, an honor apparently bestowed on those who actually accept and pay for the items they win. Besides my prestigious track record as a dependable buyer, I'd quickly found unique gifts for nearly everyone on my list.

"I'm halfway to my yellow star!" I told my husband. "And *Zoobilee Zoo*: I can't believe how much time I've saved. Can you imagine how long it would have taken me to find the Kappas or the Jose Canseco figure or the Henry Cabot Lodge campaign button or the 1994 VHS tape of *Zoobilee Zoo* if I hadn't learned how to bid?"

He seemed unimpressed.

"And," I added, "I've saved so much money!"

"I know," he said, "but we seem to be talking more about how much you've saved than how much you've spent."

That, of course, is a mere detail we have not completely explored. Suffice to say that I was slightly less honest than the Kappa seller. When I logged on just minutes before the auction ended, I learned that my $20 maximum had been outbid, but I did ultimately win the pants. And that's all I'm telling.

Not all of us attended Yale Divinity School.

Volunteering to Simplify Is Complicated

It's probably not a great time to bring this up. Aunt Agnes just roared in from Tennessee with a gift-wrapped turkey fryer in her trunk, and Uncle Hal is so proud of the red-flannel electronic foot massager he brought.

But once the gift bags and paper crinkles are cleared from the family room floor, where is all this stuff going to live?

Facing the holiday glut, I decided a while back that the way to figure this out was to take a little one-nighter called "Introduction to Voluntary Simplicity." The course description made it sound easy and wise.

"Voluntary simplicity," read the brochure, "involves both inner and outer condition. It means singleness of purpose, sincerity and honesty within, as well as avoidance of exterior clutter, of many possessions irrelevant to the chief purpose of life. … It involves a deliberate organization of life for a purpose."

I was momentarily awed.

But the evening the class was scheduled, I seemed to have organized my life more around getting dinner on the table than getting to class at 7.

"I'll eat on the way," I yelled, grabbing a banana as the computer spit out driving directions. "I'm off to change my life."

During a MapQuest moment or two, I imagined that the other students, who had probably arrived early, were all simply attired, probably in black, sitting yoga-style on a highly polished wooden floor either deep-breathing or reading *Walden*.

But by the time I rushed in, they were just sitting at those little books-on-the-bottom school desks and confessing.

"We came," announced one couple solemnly, "because clutter is an issue in our relationship." They threw each other looks.

"His clutter," she said, "is his books. There's no place for them all."

"Her clutter," he said, "is her cat. Also, the oven because she never uses it."

"You could put your books in my oven," she said.

"You could put your cat …"

But before it got more interesting, the instructor passed out something called a "Fulfillment Curve Exercise."

"One person's clutter," she said, "is another person's comfort. Mentally, go though your possessions and rank them: Survival, Comfort, Luxury or Clutter. You'll find that the closer they get to survival needs, the more satisfaction you get from your things."

Even the most directionally impaired could see where this was going. I fit the car, the washing machine, the dryer, the dishwasher, the TV, the PC, the Palm Pilot, the cell phone, the fax machine, the laptop, the answering machine, my watch, the food processor, the toaster oven and the piano all in the Survival column.

The treadmill and the exercise mat, which take up way too much space, went into Clutter.

Everything looked good until the instructor asked us to share our results, and an attractive, simply dressed, middle-aged woman in the back of the room raised her hand.

I don't remember all that she said, but I know it came around to this final statement: "More than six pairs of shoes is a luxury."

Six pairs of shoes? I'm not sure whether I was the only one there with a little Imelda secret in the closet, or whether a voluntary simplicity class is not exactly the place to start counting and announcing. But no one said a word.

I, for one, had many questions, and unless I sign up for the full eight-session course and run into the Shoe Lady again, I will probably never know …

Do you have to count every season at once? Beach shoes? Garden clogs? Old running shoes? Vinyl boots from college? What about free slipper socks from the hospital that have never been worn? And does a person with only six pairs ever get to wear red?

I might throw out a few pairs if they count. Or send them out to my teething granddog, who can make quick work of a pair of high heels.

Maybe a couple more minutes in Uncle Hal's red flannel electronic foot massager would help me decide. I'm certainly keeping that little survival machine.

How could something that runs on batteries and has the feet stuck together possibly be a pair of shoes?

Leash Laws

Gloves. They belong in pockets or on hands. Those two places only. Not on the next chair or on your lap in the car. Remember that, and never again waste time hunting.

Umbrellas. Let them hang on the same hanger that's holding the coat that's sporting the pockets that are holding the gloves.

Long fingernails. They're great for impersonating a lady of leisure. Enjoy the break. But for more enduring enjoyment, try a massage manicure and some clear polish. It's less expensive and more relaxing, and you can still open a beer.

Mooms. If you are the mother of the groom, do not try to compete with the mother of the bride. It's hopeless. Instead, enjoy the anonymity and thank God you are neither counting the Jordan almonds nor paying for them. Besides, you have just saved yourself 1,456 hours of wedding planning.

Shoes. Don't worry about having more than six pairs of shoes. Don't even worry about counting them. But if your closet is jammed with shoes you never wear, that hurt your feet or look like those free slippers they give out at the hospital, grab yourself a garbage bag and toss them in. Then head for your favorite charity. You'll help your feet, someone else's feet and, assuming your clodhoppers are in "used or better" condition, your tax return. You'll also save pawing time locating your favorites in a better organized closet.

Duds. Travel clothes, easily available through online sources such as http://www.travelsmith.com/ and http://www.magellans.com/, are good timesavers because they feature wrinkle-free, no-iron fabrics that can be tossed in the washer and dryer or hung to dry. Their neutral mix-and-match combos, like black and khaki, not only make packing easier but also reduce the number of pieces you have to jam in your closet at home. With less stuff, your closet can be easier to navigate, with or without tons of closet organizing aids.

eBay. It's a dog that can devour tons of your time and money, but it can be a huge time and money-saver, too. If you have gambling ways, Las Vegas rules apply. Set a dollar limit before starting to bid, and go shopping with the *Buy It Now* or maximum bid features. Then go take a walk. Or many walks if the remaining time is long. Not to worry. If you're the winner, you'll get that e-mail asking for your payment .

Chapter Four

Not What the Doctor Ordered

Illness is a dog that can swallow a planner whole. Whether it's a "sick call" from the school nurse or the midnight call from an aide at mom's nursing home, sudden illness trumps all other priorities.

Add to the emergencies all those regimens for illness prevention, and voila! — there are only 11.2 minutes of personal time left in the average day.

It's No Fun Keeping Weight Off

There's nothing wrong with me. Never mind that in the last few weeks I've locked my car keys in the trunk, paged myself repeatedly to find the pager, phoned myself repeatedly to find the cell phone and become the lucky recipient of several ominous notices from the library and video store.

This has nothing to do with old age or early confusion. It's just that my husband, already suffering from a bad back, had the audacity to zig instead of zag, twist instead of turn, and very decidedly broke his left foot.

It would be one thing if all he usually did was click the remote, but this is a guy who normally schleps kids to the mall, helps buy the groceries and does his own laundry. Ground him for a few days, and life gets disturbing. Ground him for a few months, and you've got a cell phone playing Beethoven's Fifth under the living room couch.

The craziness started in the examining room.

"Just wear this," the doctor said, tossing an enormous Velcro boot my husband's way.

"And," he added, "absolutely no weight on that foot. It's in a bad spot, but if you stay off it for a few months, it'll eventually heal."

A few months? I gulped.

"So how do you suddenly *do* that in a two-story house?" I asked the good doctor. "How do you absolutely put no weight on your foot?"

He looked at me blankly and uttered one of those cryptic medical pronouncements that — to put it politely — left the details up to us.

"It's not my job to tell you how," he said. "It's just my medical recommendation."

The next few days were a blur. Suffice it to say that we quickly became the proud custodians of a wheelchair, a pair of wooden crutches, an electric stairlift that obliterates half the staircase, several easy-to-reach files capable of holding the hundreds of insurance claim forms that were headed our way, and — since he was able to do some of his work from home in an upstairs office — a new refrigerator, toaster and coffee pot.

In a world where orthopedic disaster interrupted everyday chaos, I immediately started groping for some new division of labor.

To my credit, I created an impressive list of tasks it is possible to do while putting absolutely no weight on one's left foot.

These include sitting — while folding clothes, cutting up baked chicken, snapping green beans, filling out insurance forms, reviewing the reasons the forms have been rejected, writing back and writing back again.

To his credit, he has done them and — with the exception of developing elaborate conspiracy theories about insurance companies and health care providers — has done them without complaint.

To my credit, I have discovered that six packs of pop-top V-8 and tuna in vacuum-packed bags can avert starvation when a certain person forgets to stock the upstairs refrigerator. And to his credit, he has actually consumed them.

All in all, except for a few misplaced and unreturned items, we are happy to report to the rest of the Velcro-footed world that the doctor's recommendation is possible to follow.

In fact, during the last visit the doctor seemed pleased.

"Coming along just fine," he said, with a contemplative-sounding *hmm* or two as he thumbed through a thickening file.

"Keep it up," he said, "and before you know it, you'll be well enough for back surgery."

Please.
No More Great Material

There are two disconcerting things about writing a humor column. One is that no matter what disaster befalls me, my friends can see the humor in it.

Laid over 36 hours at the Dubuque Airport?

"Wow!" they say. "What a great column!"

Tied up in traffic for an hour and a half?

"Great material!" they tell me.

Unfortunately, the challenge in writing a column once a month has not been finding material but picking which particular disaster stands above the rest. Take June. Please.

The family reunion looked like a promising source: 25 relatives converging on us from all over the country. Since the gathering was my husband's idea, it fell to him to coordinate flights, orchestrate airport runs and plan a menu that fit everyone's budgets and special diets. This was the same week our daughter was shopping and packing for eight weeks of overnight camp.

"Where do you buy pink legumes?" he wanted to know, surveying the yard-long organic recipe his sister had sent from California. "And how can seven people use the same rental car when they're arriving on different flights?"

"I can't pick them up," our daughter said. "I'm packing."

"Me neither," I said. "I'm working."

So it was around the time that cousin Suzy from Helotes, Texas, was driving the family rental between the state park lodge — and not, fortunately, when I was behind the wheel — that The Mega Disaster struck. The reunion-planner's right leg, long plagued with diabetic ulcers, was infected and had to go.

"This is not good timing," my husband said, making the understatement of the year. "This is not good at all."

Still, he bravely persevered through the pre-amputation Sunday lunch for 25 at our house and the planting of a tree in memory of his 98-year-old dad, who had died two months earlier.

The tree was barely planted before he hatched Disaster No. 3. This was the notion that somehow we should freeze the limb in case he ever needed it for, say, a lawsuit against the insurer, who refused to authorize further treatments for the infection.

"I think an Orthodox Jewish funeral home would do this," he said, "because I think you are supposed to save all your body parts and bury them at once."

"You are not Orthodox," I pointed out. "You eat ham, and you hardly know the difference between Rosh Hashanah and Yom Kippur."

"Besides," our daughter said, "the jurors would be grossed out. They wouldn't pay you a dime."

The thought of waving the frozen leg in front of a jury, though, seemed to propel him through the surgery, which the doctor announced "went beautifully" as he proceeded to share the technical aspects of severing a leg below the knee.

Happy in the belief that bad luck comes only in three's, I immediately called my mother, who at 87 conducts prayer vigils for ailing relatives. Known as The Family Pipeline, she is charged with warding off catastrophic complications like brain damage on behalf of those who undergo even simple appendectomies.

"You did a great job, mom," I told her. "The surgery went fine."

A weak and disoriented voice answered, followed by a bone-crushing cough that did not return from the depths for a good 15 seconds.

"Too much cold air," she gasped, referring to a period of some 75 minutes when someone's failure to order the no-cheese pizza for lactose-intolerant family members had left her chilled in the reunion picnic shelter.

Long story short, within 24 hours she and my husband were conspiring to share the same hospital room, but it was determined that pneumonia and congestive heart failure were not a good mix with the recently dismembered.

At the beginning, I mentioned that there are two disturbing things about writing a humor column. For anyone still waiting, the other is that there is always someone out there who will read about a good disaster and want to know, "Did that really happen? Is that really true?"

And to that person, I must confess: I never waited 36 hours at the Dubuque Airport.

Visits to Doctor
Can Cause Headaches

I used to think it was an accomplishment to make and keep a medical appointment.

First, there was not losing the little card that came in the mail. And then actually putting it in my purse. Then remembering to call the number at some time other than my lunch hour, when the doctor's office was closed. And then waiting on the line till the nurse picked up the call.

When I did get through, there was finding a time other than the always available 10:30 a.m., when half a day's work would be disrupted. And finally escaping from the office in time to walk to the car, navigate traffic, show up and read for awhile about Michael Jackson's latest nose job. Altogether, a nine-step program.

That was in the good old days. A few weeks ago, after I scribbled my name on the clipboard list outside the little glass door, the receptionist presented me with an entire training program for going to the doctor.

"Here," she said. "Read these." With that, she handed me a typewritten yellow sheet and a typewritten pink sheet and pointed to a rack of nice-looking brochures about the rising cost of professional liability insurance. I think this was in place of "Good morning."

One brochure made the worrisome observation that a heart surgeon might not be immediately available if I had a heart attack.

The yellow sheet nearly gave me one. "Prescription Notification To Our Patients," it read. And in four styles of very large dark type, it listed more rules than a business casual dress code for the business of getting a prescription. What caught my eye was the dollar sign. If I goofed, it would cost me $5.

The pink sheet explained annual exams, but there were no

dollar signs, so I skipped back to the yellow.

A quick look told me two things: Marcus Welby did not write these, and I may not be organized enough to keep going to the doctor.

The yellow sheet said to take my prescription and go directly to a pharmacy when I left. "This way, it will not get lost while you use the samples given at your visit."

I suppose that makes more sense than leaving the prescription on some lunch counter or under the front seat of the car. But then it got complicated.

It went on to say both that prescriptions are valid up to six months from the date they are written and that they are typically written for a year's worth of refills valid for a year from the date they are written but that I would have to initiate their use within six months and a phoned-in extension would cost an extra $5. Already, I am lost and wondering whether one of those Internet greeting card services would mind sending me a get-well card on all the appropriate dates.

The pink annual exam sheet turned out to be the sleeper, though. Fortunately, I had time to read it before climbing on the exam table and answering any questions like "How have you been?"

Seems that if there were "issues" I needed to discuss that day, beyond prescription refills and a couple of standard exam procedures, I'd have to reschedule the exam because "your insurance carrier will not pay for the expense of both of those services on the same day."

The form did not say whether the forms themselves were an issue that could be discussed, or whether it was OK to talk about the state of Michael Jackson's nose or the chaotic state of one's life that made it so difficult to get there in the first place. It appeared that bunions would definitely trigger the nine steps required to make a second appointment.

So when the doctor finally arrived, flashing a Marcus Welby smile and spewing the usual questions, I was on guard. "So how are things going?"

"Terrific!" I said.

"How's the family"

"Just great!"

"Staying busy?"

"That's another issue," I laughed, catching myself just in time. "I mean life is great."

"So any questions?"

"Just one." I said, hopping down and heading for the door. "Do you have a couple of Tylenol? I seem to have developed a terrible headache."

Flossing Could Be Heart-Felt Exercise

It was on the eve of my dental appointment, just after brushing furiously to erase six months of sins, that I made the confession.

"Sometimes," I told my husband, "I get too busy to floss."

A military-style flosser who lines the bathroom sink with brushes and mint-flavored waxed flosses and a special mouthwash he orders online, he blanched. "It's more important than brushing!" he said.

I turned to my usually sympathetic mother, who's accepted the slimy pre-peeled carrots and browning salad bags that make dinners at our house a snap.

"I just don't have time," I explained.

"Patricia!" she said.

I have not been called Patricia since I was 9 and had my allowance docked for failing to scrub the ring out of the tub.

But the hygienist the next morning topped them both. "They've found a link," she said, "between gum disease and stroke."

Drooling, with two latex gloves in my mouth and some sort of plaque-blaster vibrating against a molar, it was hard to argue and easy to imagine the worst.

While she had a captive audience, she went on. "They've found that people with certain kinds of bacteria in their mouths have the thickest carotid arteries," she said, "and that when this bacteria enters the circulatory system, it can contribute to heart disease."

She called the bacteria "mean and vengeful" and flipped open a tooth-shaped board book. It contained the rottenest-looking pictures of a mouth I've seen since the ones I taped to the bathroom mirror when my boys were in high school and sneaking chewing tobacco at the gas station.

I took her comments in stride until a few days later when the *New York Times* took up the campaign with an article called "Flossing Can Be a String to the Heart." The article said the same thing as the hygienist, only it quoted a professor at Columbia University.

"It's not yet been proved," he hedged, but hinted that using 15 or so yards of floss a day was probably not a bad idea.

It may turn out in the end that the study was funded by some dental floss manufacturer and that too much flossing actually leads to brain damage in rats, but it seems risky to ignore recommendations coming from such a high level.

"It's one thing to be eulogized as a workaholic who had a heart attack," I told my husband. "Quite another for your tombstone to say you didn't floss. I'm in."

He seemed pleased that I'd purchased an electric toothbrush with a blue-flashing charge light that matches his, along with extra heads and several styles of floss. I drew the line at the mail-order mouthwash and lugged home a huge bargain bottle of green-colored solution that promised to fight bacteria and prevent the ugly gum disease gingivitis.

"It won't take that long," he promised. "Not even 10 minutes a day."

He's probably right. But I'm still new at this, and I want to follow perfectly the illustrated "Proper Flossing Technique" instructions I found on the Web.

"I'm figuring 20 minutes a day," I told him, "just to be sure."

"Anyone can find 20 minutes a day," he said.

He's absolutely right, of course. I just knocked it off my exercise routine.

My Health Care Plan Unveiled

We hear a lot these days about health care plans and the nuances among them. Every candidate has a point of view and so does every voter.

With so much at stake here, I'd be doing the country a disservice if I didn't advance my own agenda for health care. Not for providing it, but for surviving the system we've already got.

But first, like the candidates, I should reassure readers that I am an expert on the subject.

I started my health care journey when the children were small and the phone rang not at 3 a.m. but at work, normally in the middle of a critical meeting.

"Ahhhh!!!!!" shrieked a child, which was another way of saying: "Drop everything and rush me to the ER." Thanks to the middle son, who struggled with the concept of cause and effect, I earned a frequent flyer card to the ER by sixth grade along with suspicious glances from the admitting staff.

When the last of the three went off to college, I thought my crisis days were done. But like once-quiet siblings, my husband and mother quickly stepped in to fill the void.

I can't go to the grocery store without running into a nurse, tech or social worker who's worked on one of them. I recognize them everywhere, even in their civilian clothes.

"You do amazing blood draws," I gush while I'm scouring the pasta aisle for low-sodium tomatoes. "He didn't have a single bruise."

And I mean it. Most hospital personnel are hard-working, competent and giving. But hey, the system is stressed, and every once in a while (usually on the day of admission), there's a TV special on infants who were given adult doses of blood thinner by mistake and bled from every orifice. So it makes sense to get educated in the ways of health care.

For those who are lucky enough to be novices, here's my health care plan:

Buy a red file folder for every member of the family. Walking into the ER with one is impressive if it bulges with copies of insurance cards (if you are lucky enough to have any), living wills, health care powers of attorney, signed Do Not Resuscitate orders, and lists of medications, allergies, and every surgical procedure the patient has ever had.

Jam enough food, water, reading material, electronic devices, dollar bills and change into a tote bag to sustain you for 18 to 24 hours. This is how long it may take to get the patient admitted or discharged. Don't forget the charger cord for your cell phone and a stack of Post-It notes on DayGlo paper. If the tote bag happens to say "American Academy of Trial Lawyers," so much the better.

Don't be shy about advocating for your patient — even the admissions booklet tells patients to "Speak Up. Help Prevent Errors in Your Care" — and to bring along a trusted friend as an advocate. In other words, the patient, who's partly done himself in with the lawnmower or a medication error, is supposed to keep the doctor from finishing the job. And the trusted friend, who's driven the half-comatose patient to the hospital, is supposed to save both the patient and the doctor from themselves.

It never hurts to ask if anyone has ordered the patient's usual 16 medications before he is admitted overnight and to check and be sure that all of the allergies in the file are actually written on the patient's plastic bracelet, not just the ones that fit on a single bracelet. Remind the hospital that they are allowed to attach multiple bracelets. Our personal best is three.

Before leaving your charge (and after 18 hours or so, you will be ready), ask what phone number's on file for you. If the patient has ever been in the system before, don't be surprised if after playing 20 questions with the admitting desk, the number is still from your first job after high school. Give them your current one. Then write it on a DayGlo sticky note. Then apply it to the front of the chart.

Stumble on back to your car, but not before finding out the name of the assigned nurse and the phone number for the desk.

70

That way, if the patient has not answered the bed phone for several hours and you imagine him sprawled across the floor, you can beg someone to go check.

All this said, I must admit that my health care plan may not be universal. It is limited to my experience, generous as it is. In the interest of universal health care, please step up and share your own hospital stories by entering them on my blog, *The Dog Journal*, at http://www.PatSnyderOnline.com/journal. The nation will be in your debt.

Leash Laws

Mega medical disasters. Medical disasters are bound to hit en masse for anyone who's caring for several family members. For sandwich generation caregivers, who have responsibility for parents, kids as well as themselves and spouses, the odds of mega disasters increase exponentially. Contrary to my shining example, this is not the time to host a family reunion, prom party or welcoming party for the new neighbors. Instead, cut back to the bare essentials, enlist paid and/or volunteer help and schedule a block of just-for-you time every day. By the way, screaming in the shower also helps.

Minor medical disasters. After a few mega disasters, it is tempting to say, "I have no life! I am always canceling my plans!" A word of warning. Cutting back to the bare essentials applies only to *mega* disasters. Adults and teens felled by sprains and garden-variety ailments can often fend for themselves and even take on some sedentary household tasks in their weakened condition. Studies (my own) show that folding and filing are three times more therapeutic than watching *Days of Our Lives*. Special note: Although cutting back to the bare essentials is not required for minor disasters, scheduling a block of personal time for yourself each day is.

Doctor visits. It's no secret that physicians sometimes burn out in the struggle to reconcile good medical care with the demands of today's health care industry. Chronically long waits for care, rushed visits and lack of familiarity with a patient's file can all be symptoms that something is amiss. If candid discussion doesn't improve the doctor-patient relationship and quality of care, it may be time to find a doctor who's more in tune.

Post-surgery strategies for patients. My mom had simple words for anyone just home from the hospital: *Keep your PJs on.* She knew that as soon as the patient emerges from the bedroom fully clothed, he becomes the perfect candidate to empty the dishwasher, inflate some bike tires and, after a day or so, clean the gutters. And those are only the demands from other family members. The over-ambitious patient will invent his own to-do list. So mom was right. Plan to do nothing, and dress for the occasion.

Flossing and other mouthy ideas. Floss!! Do it!! It works!! Now that we've resolved that question, let's move on to the latest recommendation from my friendly hygienist: daily tongue-cleaning. It seems that those with so-called "geographic," or groovy, tongues are especially susceptible to breeding anaerobic bacteria that cause bad breath and the dreaded "white tongue." From the looks of the pictures of tongues posted on the Internet (who poses for these?), it's important to run, not walk, to the dentist to pick up a free plastic tongue scraper. What's one more minute when you're already flossing?

Hospital stays. Thanks to readers who responded to *My Health Care Plan Unveiled* with their personal stories, here are a few reader-suggested tips for hospital survival:

> Don't forget your laptop.
> Don't forget the charger cord for your laptop.
> Don't forget the patient.

Chapter Five

The Stress of Stress Relief

Nothing can stir up stress like advice about relieving it. Whether it's a 400-page book with illustrations, 59 magazine tips that must be read before the bagger sacks the groceries or simply friendly advice, a barrage of stress relief strategies can be mind-numbing.

Maybe it would be better if the dog had eaten the how-to books instead of the planner.

Life Is a Series of Open Loops

It was a well-meaning gift, the little paperback called *Getting Things Done.*

"It sounds good, don't you think?" asked my friend Mary as she handed it to me on Christmas Day. "I especially like the subtitle: *The Art of Stress-Free Productivity.*"

"Yes!" I said with genuine enthusiasm. "I could use some stress relief."

I couldn't help but notice that the author, who was billed by one corporate exec as "my personal productivity guru," looked relaxed but supremely well-groomed on the cover. He wore a black suit, starched white shirt and tasteful red tie. His teeth were perfectly spaced, his hair was perfectly cut and his stylish wire-rimmed glasses perfectly sparkled.

Despite his own spit and polish, he pledged to help me "feel fine about what you're *not* doing."

"I like this guy already," I told her, and I began to troll through the 259 pages that David Allen promised would put me in the "ready state of the martial artist." The goal, he said, was to develop a "mind like water," like a still pond. Then when a pebble was thrown in, I would respond "appropriately to the force and mass of the input and then return to calm."

I happily assumed we were off on a don't-sweat-the-small-stuff-and-it's-all-small-stuff trip when the guru took a nasty turn. He began discussing how each undone thing in my life needed to be collected and placed on a massive list with action steps so it was not distracting me from my "ready state."

"Every open loop," he said, "must be in your collection system and out of your head." It was so important that he suggested setting aside a period of 14 hours to get started. During this time, I was supposed to plan how to "do, delegate or defer" each loop that was "actionable" and "trash, incubate or reference" each one that was not. If I did this correctly, he promised, I would achieve the ultimate productive state: I would become as productive as most people are the week before they go on a vacation.

I thought a Friday night would be a good time to announce this project to my family.

"I just need a couple of days off to list all the undone things in my life and figure out what to do about them," I said. "I should be done by the end of the weekend."

Immediately, they rushed in to help.

"One would be groceries," my daughter suggested, staring at the empty shelves in the fridge. "Light bulbs," added my husband. "Put that on the list. And while you're out, we could use some extra furnace filters."

"You just don't get it," I said. "I won't be doing anything for the next 14 hours except listing and planning. It's the only way I can empty my head."

Whatever they may have felt at that moment about my head and the need to empty it, they did, to their credit, allow the collection process to proceed.

"How's it going?" my husband asked after a couple of hours.

"I can't stop listing," I said, feeling more stressed with every loop. "One loop seems to lead to another."

Before bedtime, I was up to 26 personal open loops, including organizing home office supplies and making pre-need funeral arrangements. We still had no groceries, and I hadn't even started on the professional loops I was supposed to list for work.

Just in case I forgot anything, the book included a "triggers" list of at least 100 words — like "phones" and "civic issues" and "vacations" — that could remind me of more loops that I didn't even know were in my head but needed to be emptied anyway.

Eventually, I suppose I will make friends with my now-more-than-247 open loops and start the associated action steps. Then, I'm sure I will relax, my mind will be like water and I will be able to respond appropriately to any pebbles that come my way.

But until then, I'm taking the first action step under vacations: going on one. Not that I need it. I just want to be highly productive the week before.

Five Big Rocks
Make Quadrants a Quandary

It was one of those introspective thoughts that circles all year around women's groups and comes in for a landing in January.

"I've got my life down to five big things," Nan announced. "And everything else is nothing. Just five big things. Now I have time for what's important."

She added that her husband, who happened to be one of the big five, had sighed and said: "About time."

The rest of us, fresh from drafting our New Year's resolutions, squinted politely and kept quiet. All but Tonya, who said Nan's comment reminded her of the jar with the rocks.

"You know. The Stephen Covey thing. You have this big jar and all this sand and all these pebbles and some water and some big rocks." She paused, her eyes circling the room.

"If you don't put the big rocks in first, you can't get the rest in."

"Aaah!" we said between bites of chocolate chip pie.

Then someone broke the sugar spell with a sharper, more threatening thought.

"Let's all bring in rocks next month! Five rocks apiece! One for each important thing in our lives. And we have to tell what it is."

No one else seemed to flinch. But like a true-false test with five 20-pointers, the exercise seemed troubling during dessert, confusing on the way to the car and completely daunting by the time the garage door went up.

I collared my husband and explained the problem. "Is it OK to have one rock called 'family'? Or does there need to be a rock for each person? And if there does, haven't I almost used mine up with a husband and three kids? And what about my mom?"

He shrugged as if I'd come looking for a pair of lost shoes.

"Sorry," he said, "I don't know what to tell you."

The obvious source was Stephen Covey himself, so I dug through my private stash of self-help books. One of them, I knew, had the jar that Tonya had remembered.

Sure enough, on page 89 of a blue-and-red volume was a sketch of a pitiful little jar filled up to its neck with water, pebbles and sand. And on page 90, the triumphant jar with several big rocks, water, pebbles and sand.

The sketches were tucked in a chapter called "Quadrant II Organizing," which explained that everything we do belongs in one of four "quadrants." It said that by paying attention, it is possible to make time for important but not urgent (Quadrant II) activities like relationships, prevention and values clarification. The big rocks.

Quadrant II activities, it seemed, should sometimes trump those in Quadrant I, which were urgent and important, like deadlines and crises. And most times, they would hopefully also trump those in Quadrant III (urgent but not important) as well as those in the dreaded Quadrant IV (not urgent and not important either), like watching too much TV or taking "some" phone calls.

By the end of the chapter, I was still confused about whether every family member was a rock. And I was in a quandary over quadrants. And I wondered which phone calls we were talking about and how much TV.

For example, what if I watched a really bad movie (Quadrant IV, time-waster) that I'd heard was uplifting (Quadrant II, empowerment) with a friend (Quadrant II, relationships) that wasted her time too (Quadrant IV, trivia) but that we talked about afterwards (Quadrant II, values clarification).

Could a bad movie become a big rock?

To make matters worse, the book's sample calendar pages showed several different Quadrant II events every day. This could mean a jar for every day of the week, different rocks in every jar, all of which would be too heavy to carry to the meeting.

As with most of life's dilemmas, the solution was obvious: Shopping (Quadrant II, true recreation).

With a brand new planner ($51.93) to go with my Palm Pilot, I acquired not only a calendar but a "weekly compass" in a see-through pocket that had a place for listing the big rocks of the week, all printed on paper with beautiful pastel pictures of the seasons of the year.

I still don't know how to use it. Every time I try, the pictures of yellow snow-capped tulips and sun-kissed blueberries urge me to forget what's on the schedule and go take a walk.

I don't know if a walk is a rock, but it's the best self-help I know.

Flying Light in the War on Paper

It's an environmentalist's dream, the woven milk crate beside the desk in our home office.

"Looks like straw, but it's recycled paper," I point out to anyone who'll listen. "What's perfect is that we use it to recycle junk mail."

The truth is, although I'd like to look like a high-minded poster child for the Sierra Club, I have selfish motives. The milk crate is a weapon in my war on paper. Once a sheet creeps in our filing systems, it dwells for as long as a Styrofoam cup in a landfill. Forever.

It's not that I think cleaning out files is unimportant. I've read that no matter how chaotic the schedule, purging them should be a priority. In fact, it's supposed to be freeing.

"A release from the past," one authority called it, "a nudge toward the future." When my files are finally cleaned out, she went on to say, I'd be able to "fly light and unencumbered." When they are finally....

But somehow, a couple of inches into a folder, fingers flying, a small voice pipes up.

"As soon as you throw me away, you will need me," it says.

Or in a more menacing tone, "You will forget to shred a credit card number and spend the next six years of your life fending off charges for a pair of Ferragamos you never owned."

My husband is no help. A piler instead of a filer, he prides himself on the ability to extract a single sheet from a spot two-thirds down a stack of seemingly unrelated papers.

"What can I say?" he asks, producing the requested receipt for carpet cleaning performed in the fall of 2001. "It works."

Because the piles are, as he says, chronologically grouped (each paper having been stacked on the next one at a time), it would cause havoc to eliminate a sheet or two, or three or more.

"Leave them alone," he says clearly. And so, until they list to one side and swoosh to the floor, I am left to attack only my own collection, which inhabits bulging folders with unenlightening names ("miscellaneous," for example).

This need not be unpleasant, I've read. "Reward yourself," instructed one organizing guru on the Web. "Make the experience something you look forward to." I believe the specific recommendation was to play classical music. But I assumed that any reward would do and gained five pounds cleaning out two file drawers and eating two quarts of Chunky Monkey.

When the season finales started up, I hauled our files in front of the TV and purged my way through a sea of suspense, thanks to *The Office*, *Boston Legal*, *Lost* and *Scrubs*. Before I found out whether George left Calliope for Izzie on *Grey's*, I'd winnowed a bankers box full of warranties down to a handful of folders. The George episode was so gripping that I hope we still have paperwork for the washer and dryer.

Our latest incentive for file attack is a newly discovered gadget: the home label maker. Complete with keyboard and screen, it spits out crisp, professional labels with peel-off backs.

Imagine the look of a file drawer, contents sleekly pruned, lined up in military order and labeled. Or at least labeled.

There's something quieting about a professional label on a file folder, even if its innards are bulging and in disarray.

"Everything's under control," it seems to wink. "Your secret's safe with me."

At the moment, the label maker is flying way ahead of the milk crate in the paper wars.

Don't Say There's No Time to Exercise

It started with an innocent comment.

"I feel great!" I told the doctor. "Of course, with the holidays coming, I won't have time to exercise."

I expected a lecture. Instead, she just laughed.

"We all say that," she said. "Of course, it's not true."

Before I could ask "When?" she was glibly striding down the hall. "You just hire a personal trainer and go to the gym," she called back.

"Is this before I pack my lunch at 5:30 a.m.?" I wanted to ask. "Is this instead of sleeping or washing my hair?"

But as I say, she was already down the hall and so confident in her swagger that I decided it was only right to take her up on the challenge. Many claim there is no time to exercise, but it became my mission to prove once and for all that this was true, that it was not a lack of will, discipline or enthusiasm for riding a bike at, say, 6 a.m. that made it impossible. It was simply the logistical impossibility and the hardship on my family.

"I'm going to start exercising for 45 minutes four times a week!" I told them when I got home.

"When?" they wanted to know. It was gratifying to see that those closest to me could see this was impossible.

"Probably before work," I said, adding to my daughter, "I won't be able to wake you up for school."

"Good," she said.

"Be sure and turn off our alarm completely," my husband added. "Don't just hit Snooze."

Their response was disheartening. No one even raised the need for me to bring in the paper at 7, empty the dishwasher or set out the dinner ingredients on the counter by the sink.

"I'll be leaving in a rush," I said. "You'll be on your own."

They appeared unfazed by the news, so I left to dig a gym bag from the bowels of the basement, remember a lock combination I hadn't used in three-and-a-half years, pack shower shoes and underwear in Ziploc bags, and run out to the store for a duplicate set of makeup.

"The plan," I explained, "is that I'll put everything in the car the night before, roll out of bed at 5, get straight into my gym clothes, eat an oatmeal bar on the way, work out for 45 minutes, shower, get dressed, eat a banana in the car and be downtown by 8."

"Sounds like a plan," my husband said, again mentioning the Snooze button.

"I won't be back to remind you when school starts," I warned our daughter.

"Good," she said.

The first day, I could tell that while the routine might be seamless at home, there could be trouble ahead at the gym.

That very first morning, after 45 minutes of stretching, walking, leg-curling, weight-lifting, biking and balancing myself on a large red rubber ball in a flying bird position (courtesy of the personal trainer), there were only three hair-dryer plugs for four working women. The other three, already plugged in, had enough long tresses and hair gel to attend the bride at a Hollywood wedding.

"I was hoping to come before work," I moaned to the desk attendant, "but I obviously can't get out in time." I could hardly wait to mention this to the doctor.

"Lots of other plugs here," he offered, pointing out 14 other options.

My boss was no less helpful, commenting that I could flex in later and stay later because "after all, I'm a fan of physical fitness." Staying later was not altogether appealing.

"I may be coming home a little later," I told our daughter. "I won't be able to remind you about homework."

"Good," she said.

I must reluctantly confess that other obstacles have also disappeared. When I forgot the shampoo and used body wash instead, my hair — fortunately or not — looked about the same. And when I wore one black and one navy sock to work, no one seemed to notice.

But I'm not ready to give in yet and say this is doable.

"Wait 'til it's icy and snowy," my mother said. "Might not be possible then."

A hopeful thought, mom. Finally, something to like about winter.

"Vision Board" a Must for Retirement

I must confess. Whenever the laundry's behind, the refrigerator reeks and the heels of all my shoes are run down, I've known exactly why.

"It's not possible," I've told my family, "to do it all and work full-time. Add it up. Grocery shopping, errand-running, school events, doctor's appointments, plus 40 hours-plus and a commute. Nobody can do it all!"

But now the moment of truth has come. After working more years than I'd care to admit (except to those who calculate public pensions), I have retired from my day job with the state to follow my bliss.

"Wow!" our daughter said.

I was expecting the politically correct response ("You're *way* too young"), but instead came a frightening one.

"Now you'll have time for the things you said you always wanted to do. Like clean out the basement," she said.

I've read that baby-boomers tend to spend more time figuring out if they can afford to retire than figuring out what they'll be doing once they do.

That's because there's nothing to figure. We have a 30-year backlog of moldy carrots, dirty shoes, unread books, unwatched movies and boxes that haven't been opened since we moved two houses ago in 1974.

Besides that, we have visionaries to help us plan our time. On the first day of my "retirement," I bumped into a friend who's writing a book on treasure mapping. She showed me how I could clip old magazines and create a "vision board" for following my bliss.

Within days, I'd created a foam board that showed me meditating, writing books and business plans, taking amazing trips abroad, and drifting in a hot air balloon over the Red Rocks of Sedona. ("Imagine it and it will happen," she said.)

Between tackling the backlog and envisioning the future, I entered "retirement" as an over-achiever, rounding each corner at breakneck speed.

I was thrilled at how quickly the treasure mapping worked. I had no sooner pasted the Red Rocks to the foam board than my oldest son asked whether I'd drive with him and my granddog to Phoenix, where he and his wife are relocating.

The granddog mission sounded urgent. "Winston's in transition," he explained, "so he's feeling confused. He needs to sit on your lap." Eerily, the cross-country trip would put me just hours away from the envisioned balloon ride.

Unfortunately, the Red Rock plan was soon derailed by un-envisioned complications, namely, my husband's need for emergency spinal surgery (now recovering nicely, thank you), which was scheduled just days after the middle son's wedding.

In addition, somewhere between the wedding and the surgery, I decided it was high time I washed and detailed my long-neglected car. Sure, I felt a little guilty breezing by all of the high school cheerleaders with their poster boards and suds buckets who were willing to do this for 10 bucks or so, but hey, until my bliss led me into the prosperity that's promised by all those books, I would be on a fixed income.

"Nothing to it," I announced, diving into the back seat with a Dirt Devil. This was just before I felt an un-envisioned twinge in my back, possibly related to climbing under parts of the interior I'd never before seen to catch every last French fry and paper clip.

Long story short, I was on an upholstered table days before hubby's spinal surgery, getting my knee whacked with a percussion hammer and mentally calculating that the car detailing job would run more than $300 by the time I was done.

In the end, maybe it was a bargain since the chiropractor turned out to be something of a philosopher.

"Consider this a gift," she said. "You need to let things go for awhile."

What a wise woman! Surely she wasn't referring to the Red Rocks of Sedona, though. I think she meant the basement.

Leash Laws

Getting things done. At the risk of simply adding to the stress, may I suggest a "dump list"? It's a hastily written list to dump those special projects to be tackled. For example, cleaning out the kitchen junk drawer or hall closet. Keep it handy when you're planning your day, and try to work in a small one every week, to be rewarded by — oh, I don't know — something they sell at Dairy Queen?

Setting priorities. Priorities flow from goals, and goals flow from knowing who you are and where you're going. If your priorities aren't clear, a life coach might be able to help. If you're not financially able to make that investment in yourself right now, an excellent standby book full of exercises to discern your interests and passions is Barbara Sher's *Wishcraft: How to Get What You Really Want.* Once you do the exercises, those "big rocks" may be easier to identify.

Filing and other attacks on the paper/stuff. Again, hand-holding and direction are available through professional organizers. You can locate one near you through the National Association of Professional Organizers' Web site, http://www.napo.net/Referral/ Short of hiring a professional organizer, team up with a friend or family member, and help each other through that office, basement, closet or garage guided by the written advice of professional organizers. Two how-to books that will not stress you out are Julie Morgenstern's *Organizing from the Inside Out* and Marla Dee's audiobook *Get Organized the Clear & Simple Way.* Both focus on making an organizing system work to fit your ways and needs, rather than bending your personality to fit an organizing system.

Distressing de-stressers. As with organizing, do what floats your boat, not somebody else's. And don't apologize for your de-stresser of choice. These days, with stress raging, everyone with a product seems to have a stress-relief angle. If a massage or pedicure gives you the creeps, just say no. If you hate meditation music, turn it off. Same drill if incense makes you sneeze. Maybe you'd rather catch lightning bugs. If so, poke some holes in the top of a jelly jar, and kick off your shoes.

Finding time to exercise. Like it or not, there's time. The trick is blocking out regular, reasonable periods to do a variety of exercises you like (or at least don't hate) and building exercise into everyday activities like parking farther away or walking faster. Your doctor can recommend exercises to fit your needs and abilities, and so can a personal trainer. But a friend, committed to exercising together, can be the key to keeping you on track.

The vision thing. President George H.W. Bush became famous for admitting that he lacked "the vision thing." He was not alone. In our personal lives, having no clear vision of where we're going or why can lead to frenetic activity that leads, well, nowhere. In retirement, a daily structure can pay big dividends. So can taking the time to envision what you want in this next life phase. A vision board filled with pictures of your dream life can help you sort out your priorities. No need to race pell-mell to achieve them all in the first few months, though.

Take time to laugh. Studies show that mirthful laughter, a good, old-fashioned belly laugh, can do wonders for us physically and emotionally. Join a laughter club or become a certified laughter leader (CLL) yourself so you can help others to laugh their way happy and healthy. To find a laughter club near you, or find out how to become a CLL, log on to http://www.worldlaughtertour. com.

Chapter Six

If You Can Build a House and Stay Married...

My parents built two houses together and stayed married. According to my mom, that series of events occurs in only one out of 65 million couples.

She credits their strong marriage with this achievement, specifically the fact that each is willing to give 200 percent. I remember it a little differently. In the first house, they developed such a mutual dislike for the builder that it trumped any fury they felt at each other. In the second, my mom was out of town most of the time, helping prepare my house for the arrival of grandchild No. 2. (This middle child still takes credit for saving the marriage).

As for my husband and me, no sweat. We built a house together, sold the old house and stayed married. Of course, he was recovering from multiple surgeries much of the time, lay gasping under the influence of anesthesia and painkillers, and quickly gave in to my wishes.

"Building was no big deal!" he tells our friends.

Building a House Is No Big Deal, Right?

It wasn't enough that I started a new job, shifted from part time to full time and suddenly had no time to buy groceries. On top of all that, the mortgage interest rates fell.

"This is perfect!" my husband said. "Now we can build a house!"

True, we'd been talking about wanting a first-floor master. True, my allergic husband had sent a real estate agent out for months to scout for one that had never been home to a bird or a cat or a dog. True, no such house existed in a family neighborhood in a million-mile radius.

But building? On top of everything else?

It's not such a big deal to build a house," he said, salivating over the rates. "It's not like you're building it yourself. You're working with professionals."

This did not ring true to my childhood memories. I remember my mother, veteran of two new house-raisings, saying something like, "There are so many decisions to make. If you can stay married and build a house together, you have a really good marriage."

And her friends used to comment: "Two houses? You must have an *amazing* marriage!"

So it seemed to me that "not such a big deal" was probably not such an accurate picture. But I gave in — with one condition.

"I'm not going to be one of those people who gets caught up in the details," I told him. "I just don't have time. A doorknob is a doorknob, as far as I'm concerned."

It went swimmingly for awhile, with the builder first sketching something out on a legal pad and then periodically reappearing with a large three-ring binder of instructions, which I put aside to read when I got a chance, and large sheets of tiny line drawings.

Occasionally, my mother pointed out that we seemed to be

missing something like a bedroom or a laundry chute or a clothes closet here or there, and he would draw it in. I answered the easy questions, like where the dishwasher would be going ("probably by the sink"), and before long, the frame went up.

The complications didn't start until the e-mail arrived asking, "Where are your selections?"

"What does this mean?" I asked the builder.

"You know," he said. "The cabinets. The knobs. The carpet. The appliances. The things you picked out already. Right?" He directed me to a list of vendors in the binder, scattered all around the city.

"Right!" I said, and immediately I started phoning far-flung suppliers who seemed to have only their business hours in common: 8 to 4, Monday through Friday.

"No problem!" I told my friends. "I can do this on my lunch hour."

"No way!" they said. "You need time to consider the look! The style!" I was stunned to learn that people who were not even house-hunting had opinions on the merits of brushed nickel fixtures over shiny brass ones, biscuit-colored cabinets over wood, and had lusted most of their adult lives for countertops the color of malachite.

"Read my lips," I said. "It is not that hard."

Over the next few days, I stuck to the plan. Bathroom fixtures in 45 minutes. Cabinets in a little more than an hour. My only error was taking a whole day off to pick out the floors.

"Since you have time," said the supplier, "you really should go down and see the condos this guy built. You can get the whole picture then: the floors, the cabinets, the countertops. See if the look is *you*."

This turned out to be a very bad idea. Until then, I had never thought much about brushed nickel. I went and immediately became mesmerized by the brushed nickel knobs on the kitchen cabinets and wondered whether they were more *me* than the brass ones I'd already ordered. I am quiet, not shiny.

"I think I am more of a brushed nickel person than a

brass," I confessed to my husband after much soul-searching. He called the cabinet guy and changed the knobs.

"Anything else?" he asked.

"Absolutely not," I said. "The biscuit-colored cabinets are staying, no matter what. Well, probably. And I wouldn't think of moving the dishwasher. Would you?"

Don't Be Fooled by "The Villa Vanilla"

I feel a little guilty misleading the buying public this way. Here we are, chaotically scrambling to build one house and sell another, snapping and carping at one another as we pack. But all the while, we're pretending to live in a place as serene and uncluttered as a yoga master's.

"Do we really live here?" my husband asked the other day. "With all the counters cleared and one or two coats hanging in the closets, I feel like I'm walking around in a magazine."

"I'm sick of it," our daughter groaned.

"Pick up that sock," I hissed, "and help me haul the toaster out from under the sink."

The craziness started when we invited our realtor to walk through our home and make a few suggestions to help it sell.

At first, she was polite. "Do you have really strong feelings about keeping an empty red vase on top of the speaker system?" she asked. "Could there be a better place to store six dozen pairs of tennis shoes than on a plastic boot bench in front of the TV set?"

But by the time she hit the laundry room and the linen closet, she'd started dusting and coughing and grabbing and grumping.

"This hydrogen peroxide is from 1985," she said. "Dump it before it kills you! And pack everything you're not using in boxes and label it for the move."

With that, we saluted, even though any Feng Shui expert will tell you that a red vase in the "Love and Marriage" corner of the house is good for your sex life. And proceeded to drag empty egg cartons home from the grocery and stuff them full of the 8 half-used bottles of Sno-Bowl and 16 bottles of Pine Sol that were inhabiting what the realtor said was actually the "blanket shelf" of the linen closet.

"You will be glad that you did this," she told us as she compulsively re-folded our towels and proceeded to connect us with a "home refinisher" who in three days had yanked off all my beloved wallpaper and stuffed it into six drawstring trash bags.

By the time she finished, we were living in The Villa Vanilla, colorless as a page from an unused coloring book.

"Now people can picture their *own* furniture in here," the realtor said. "And their *own* things on the countertops."

This is very good in theory, but it makes it tough to fix breakfast.

"Would they really be bothered by a toaster?" I asked. "And won't they wonder where the mixer went?"

"It looks great," she said. "Leave it alone."

I have to admit that the fridge looked better without the 47 magnets from vacation spots, the pizza coupons, the driving directions to last year's track meets and the list of foods that endanger plastic sealants on children's teeth.

The family room looks better without the boot bench. The foyer closet looks more spacious without the golf clubs and the dolly and the 16 outgrown coats we gave to the Salvation Army. And the kitchen desk looks more gracious holding up a notepad than 320 cans of pop.

But all in all, I think we're doing the public a great disservice.

"Why doesn't *your* room look like that?" some other teen's mom is apt to ask as she gazes at the clean sweep of our daughter's spotless and neutral abode (49 posters and 33 unwashed socks boxed and labeled in the crawl space).

"Why don't *we* have a blanket shelf for *our* linens?" some husband will be inclined to say.

For everyone's sake, the insanity needs to end soon.

That's why I put a message inside an empty red vase under the rocker in the "Helpful Person" corner of the living room: "Need helpful person to make an offer."

No rush. We can keep this up for at least another 15 minutes.

Yo Baby! It's Moving Day!

As we were loading up, one moving van at a time, our neighbor Roger sauntered over.

"Could never do this," he said. "Could never get all our stuff packed up and out and unpacked again."

"Oh, sure you could," I told him. "It just takes a little time."

Ten days and 597 boxes later, I think Roger is a very wise man.

Besides having all his marbles, Roger probably has all the shelves to his bookcases, the Crock-Pot to his Crock-Pot lid and all his spouse's prescription medication.

Unfortunately, I do not.

The trouble started with the innocent belief that a local move is much simpler than a long-distance one.

"After all," I told my husband, "we can take a lot of the small stuff in the car, and we always run back if we leave something behind."

One hundred-thirty-two run-backs later, I don't believe a local move is such a big advantage. With a bit more research, I would have realized that taking the back half of a huge van otherwise headed cross-country would create worries I'd never dreamed of. And with a little more planning, I would not be in the new garage now digging through garden supplies for a bottle of Amoxicillin

Of course, I'd prefer to blame the movers: a fast-moving crew of six testosterone-crazed weight-lifters who wrapped everything that wasn't breathing and jammed it all, in no particular order, into look-alike cardboard cubes. This would have been OK with an occasional label. But while their tattoos were stunning in detail, their labels said mostly "clothes" and "stuff."

"How about saying if these are women's or men's clothes?" I pleaded with one.

"I did," he said, pointing to a large X made of cellophane

tape on a wardrobe box.

"X is for men," he bellowed.

"And women?"

"No X," he said.

The rest of the day followed along those lines, with me, a mere no-X, running after six X's who hooted "Yo,baby" to each other, caught boxes mid-air and uttered to me only one complete sentence: "Where does this go, ma'am?"

The only way to keep track of the stuff leaving our old house was to stand on the front sidewalk and direct traffic. The idea was to be sure that boxes labelled "Charity" box did not get on the moving truck and that parts of the same piece of furniture all traveled together so that nothing slid away to the front of the truck and went on to Seattle. If a box or furniture part took a wrong turn, I would throw my body in front of it and scream "Nooooo!" which occasionally got their attention.

This was fine until I had to leave to go to the bathroom — an indulgence I tried to keep to a minimum — or the crew cleverly sent me on an urgent errand.

"Quick, come check the upstairs closet," Chip the Leader would yell from some distant nook of the house.

"Time to clean out the fridge," his buddy would demand, hailing me down from the stairway to dump the entire contents of the refrigerator into six picnic coolers.

"No sweat," another would say as I came back just in time to spot the edge of some charity furniture peeking out from behind the piano on the truck. "You can always run it back later," he'd say.

On the moving-in end, it worked best to direct traffic inside the front hall, sending the Yo-Baby Boys to the MBR (Master Bedroom), BR 2 (daughter's bedroom), BR3 (guest bedroom) and so on, but particularly to the unfinished side of the basement, which became the receptacle for everything from Halloween door swags to 1977 tax records to — possibly — Amoxicillin.

"It's really not so bad," I told my husband three days after the move, bleary-eyed from unpacking the kitchen till 3 a.m. Once

I washed the melted butter off the spice jars and found the oatmeal under the carpet cleaner, I knew we were almost home.

"As for the stuff in the basement, we might as well leave it packed," I told him. "Who knows? Maybe we'll be ready to downsize in a few years!"

He just glared at me, wisely. "Could never," he said, with a cough. "Could never get all this stuff packed up and out and unpacked again."

I started to argue but thought better of it. It's not nice to take on a man whose Amoxicillin just moved to the West Coast.

We're Unpacked — If You Like Your Coffee Black

Six months after a move, there's always that well-meaning person who wants to know, "Are you settled yet?"

The reply by now is automatic. "We've even hung our pictures."

Magic words. There's something about moving and hanging pictures that says life is settled.

Who, after all, would be debating where to hang their marriage vows if they were not positive where all their shoes were? Who would be centering an abstract design over the fireplace if they couldn't find the pitcher that for the past 23 years has held the coffee cream?

No one else, that's who. And so it is that for the past six months, with a picture or two on every wall, we've managed to deceive everyone who drinks their coffee black that we are, as they say, "settled." Not only unpacked but carefully organized. Not only organized but moving on handily with our lives.

The other night we were found out.

"Anything in your coffee?" I asked our neighbor.

"Just a little cream," she said.

"Actually, we don't have cream — just skim milk," I confessed.

"Nobody has cream," she said. "Not a problem."

While it was so safe to confess, I went on.

"Actually, we don't have a cream pitcher, either," I said, perilously pouring the skim milk from an orange juice glass. "I mean, it's still packed." I didn't elaborate or go so far as to conduct a tour of the basement.

But the truth is that the cream pitcher is one of many ordinary things we used to find around our house that are now stashed in our basement, hiding in a room full of boxes on the unfinished side. The fly swatter's down there somewhere. So are the barbecue tongs.

It was not supposed to be this way, but a week off work six months ago was hardly enough time to unpack the dishes and underwear. We've been stumbling sleepily behind ever since.

"Not a problem," I told my husband, "We'll do the rest a little at a time. A box a night or something."

One hundred-eighty-one nights have now passed, and the "Box a Night" plan has failed. One hundred-eighty-one boxes have not been opened. Eighty-one have not been opened. Probably 15 have not. That's because after a few nights, when it seemed more critical to do practically anything else, we switched to the "As The Need Arises" plan. The rules are simple.

"When you really need something, you go hunting for it," I explained. "The person who needs it most is in charge. And once you open a box, you have to put away the rest of the stuff."

In the past few months, we've become as spartan as monks.

"We really need a stronger light in the office," my husband commented the other night. "Don't we have some floor lamps down in the basement?"

"Several," I said, "only, the shades are boxed up." It was looking hopeful for a minute, but he quickly retreated.

"I think I'll just switch to a 100-watt bulb," he said.

There was another near breakthrough a week or so ago when the weather turned cool and our daughter couldn't find her sweatpants.

"Try the basement!" we cried in unison.

"Sorry," she said. "I'm sure I left them at summer camp."

As time goes on, we're debating whether to switch to the "If You Haven't Used It in a Year" plan recommended by veterans of not unpacking .

"If you haven't used it in a year, you probably don't need it" is the mantra. After a year, we are supposed to call the Veterans of Foreign Objects or Salvation from Excess Army to haul it all away, unopened, in exchange for a tax receipt.

The idea is alarming to my husband. "You could lose some important stuff that way!" he says. He is probably thinking of the cord to the reel-to-reel tape player he had in college.

"We wouldn't miss a thing!" I say. "And think of all the good we would do!"

Actually, I am thinking that fly swatters are cheap. And that there's no better way to start out these days than with a cup of strong black coffee.

Cabinet Space Leads to Gadge-Diction

When I first saw the kitchen cabinets at our new house, I said, "Cavernous!"

Never could we fill the treetop-high spaces designed for who-knew-what.

"Who could?" my husband asked. "You'd think we had to store the White House china."

"Plus we're all short!" our daughter complained. "You'd think we were giants."

Now 12 months later and the owner of a collapsible stepladder, I have to confess: The space is so cramped that I just hauled my tall aluminum pasta pot to the basement.

Just as housework could — theoretically, but not at our house —fill all the time available, so can kitchen gadgets fill every square inch available.

The gadget invasion has been gradual and innocent. It started as a conspiracy between clever manufacturers of "time-saving" appliances and my husband, who took an early retirement, took over the cooking, and immediately transferred his love for the Palm Pilot to an electric Spinning Salad Center.

"It's simply amazing," he said, demonstrating the ability of the 12-inch-round, electric colander to spin lettuce dry and chop vegetables at the same time. "You just feed the veggies into this little hole at the top."

It was after several months of electrically shot salads, topped with everything from tuna to chicken grilled in the 96-square-inch Grilling Machine with snap-off washable plates that I joined the craziness by purchasing a 24-inch-round quesadilla maker.

"Much simpler!" I explained. "The entire meal fits on a couple of big flour tortillas. You just throw the leftovers in between."

"What was wrong with folding little ones in half and jamming them into the sandwich maker?" our daughter wanted to know.

I had no immediate answer, but her wisdom was diluted by the fact that as she asked her question, she was feeding frozen strawberries and skim milk into a 16-inch-high Smoothie Maker. I gave her a look.

"What?" she said. "You got this for me. It's way faster than the blender where the fruit gets stuck in the bottom. Besides, what about your pancake griddle?"

I straightened. "It's more than paid for itself in instant Sunday dinners!" I said of the 19-inch-long, rectangular Teflon griddle with pull-out drip drawer. Never mind that we had also just acquired a 16-square-inch griddle that cleverly served as the non-immersible base to a countertop fry pan that would go right in the dishwasher.

"It's brilliant!" my husband cooed. "Particularly the little wire rack you can fit it in for easy storage under the sink."

With all this equipment, one simple Sunday brunch now requires a small factory full of time-saving devices: a blender for the batter, a griddle for the hotcakes, an electric skillet for the sausage, a coffee maker for the obvious, and a 20-inch-high manual juicer for the oranges.

"Life was simpler," my husband confessed, "when we had no storage space."

"You have no storage space *now*," said my mom, then a frequent Sunday dinner guest, who offered to bring a box of Eggos from the freezer of her small apartment next week.

"Brilliant!" I said. "Then we can get rid of the blender, the griddle and the immersible electric fry pan, and bring the pasta pot back upstairs."

"That would leave more than enough room for a pasta pot," she beamed. "You can bring it back up from the basement."

She's right, of course. She just hadn't figured on the companion I'd ordered for the pasta pot: a 15-pound electric PastaMatic. It makes approximately 1-1½ pounds of pasta, comes with six extruding discs (18 more by special order), a specially sized and marked liquid measuring cup, a special wrench for disc-changing, six steps of assembly instructions, 14 steps of operating instructions, and a two-page troubleshooting guide. Unfortunately, it's on back order from Italy. But I'm willing to wait.

It takes forever to run to the store for a box of spaghetti.

Leash Laws

Fixtures. If you're truly indifferent to all the little decisions that come with building, no sweat. Budget the minimum time for this process, and go with your gut. But if, like most people, you are likely to struggle with these decisions, budget time ahead — maybe a weekend for flooring, a weekend for paint colors, a weekend for plumbing fixtures — and stick to the schedule. If your builder has constructed a number of homes in the area, ask whether you can look at a few that are similar to what you've planned. Pay attention to fixtures, accessories and the overall feel of the house. Once you're ready to go shopping, call vendors for appointments and let them know your budget and the types of items you want to look at. If this process isn't fun for you, make it more bearable with lunch, dinner or dessert out afterwards.

Showings. It's easier to make the house look spacious and inviting if it has less stuff in it. Instead of trying to shove the excess into closets, try renting a storage unit for items you don't absolutely need. Some storage businesses offer the first month's rent for free, a real deal if the house sells quickly. If it doesn't and those nonessentials linger in storage for awhile, even better. You may decide to do without and donate your excess stuff to charity.

Unpacking. Do not, unless it is absolutely necessary. The one-year rule (*If you haven't used it in a year, you probably don't need it*) is a good one. Donate and rejoice! You will not be one of those people who at 70 are dealing with a 45-year accumulation.

Storage space. "I've never had a client complain there was too much of it," our builder said. But just as housework can quickly expand to fill the time allotted, so can stuff expand to fill every cabinet. Pushing your builder to include usable storage space for essentials may be more in your long-term interest than agreeing to additional hard-to-reach space.

Chapter Seven

How About a Holiday from Holidays?

No wonder special planner sections are available for getting through the holidays. The food, the gifts, the decorations can make spare time disappear faster than a bowl of puppy chow.

In our house, where we celebrate both Christmas and Hanukkah, we've turned back flips trying to figure out how to send the holidays to obedience school. We've tried delegating and simplifying, and considered giving only cash donations to charity.

The results? As mixed as Ho! Ho! Ho! and Shalom!

Holiday Sparks Skirmishes Between the Two of Me

Don't get me wrong. I'm as quick as the next to rail against commercialism.

"Hrumph!" I say to stores that open their doors at 6 a.m. the day after Thanksgiving.

"Too much!" I say to the megapounds of catalogs that slide from our mailbox with a "Hurry Now!" shout.

But the truth is, it's not the shotgun start of the ads and the catalogs that sends me running down the frantic holiday track. It's the thrill of the chase.

For the ravenous multitasker, Christmas is a feast with music and lights.

While I'd like to blame the frenzy on someone else, there's part of me that thrills to the rush of swinging by hundreds of places on the way to someplace else to pick up some little item that's listed on a sticky note flapping on the dash.

But events this fall have jolted me into thinking about what's important. Somehow, a new Simplifying Self has emerged to do battle with the Frantic One and is angling for the real spirit of the season, not just the rush and the glitz. These two parts of me are easy to distinguish and increasingly at war.

The Simplifier wears one hundred percent cotton in muted colors, very little make-up and comfortable shoes. She sips decaffeinated organic apricot tea in the glow of small vanilla candles made of pure beeswax. While meditating.

The Frantic One wears anything that's clean and makeup when she remembers, drinks lots of double espresso and loses her keys. This is while chopping tomatoes for tacos, helping with algebra and folding contour sheets with her one free hand.

It was no surprise that on a recent trip to the bookstore, a little white volume by Elaine St. James reached out, grabbed the Simplifier and coaxed her into a comfy chair in a secluded corner of the coffee bar.

After Frantic followed breathlessly and ordered a large latte, the Simplifier proceeded to absorb all 269 pages of *Simplify Your Christmas: 100 Ways to Reduce the Stress and Recapture the Joy of the Holidays*, offered by her new idol, the guru of simplifying your life.

The coffee bar exchange that followed led to the first skirmish between the two of me in this pursuit of a more spiritual holiday.

"Create a meaningful Christmas without gifts!" wrote the guru wisely.

"Human connection and no bills!" cheered the Simplifier.

"Love to shop!" cried Frantic.

"Ask family and friends not to give gifts!" the guru persisted.

"They'll be so relieved!" said the Simplifier.

"Ha! They'll think you're a Scrooge!" Frantic said.

It wasn't until we got to the DO's instead of the DON'Ts that we reached some sort of peace.

"Be unconventional!" she wrote. "Spend your Christmas money on food for the homeless."

"Much better," said the Simplifier.

"How about *part* of it?!" asked Frantic.

"Give less. Play more," instructed the guru, who then described hours of family fun that didn't require buying a thing.

"Yes," said the Simplifier.

"Buying a couple of board games couldn't hurt!" offered Frantic. "The President asked us to shop."

"Explore other traditions," the guru wrote, describing how it's customary in Finland to sprinkle straw on the dinner table to remember the humble beginnings of Christmas.

"Easier than a tree!" said the Simplifier.

"Would be nice *under* the tree!" suggested Frantic, "or around a manger scene in the front yard. Would be nice with live animals!!!"

By the bottom of the latte, the guru and myselves had simplified Christmas completely, except for identifying a working farm with a donkey on the way to a mall.

There was also the detail of whether to buy the book, listed at $14.95. But the question seemed to bring us together.

"It would make a great gift," the Simplifier said.

"Absolutely not!" said Frantic. "This year, we're cutting back."

Let's Stop Denying Men Holiday Joy

I was in my usual pre-holiday State of Overwhelm the other day when my friend Bill gave me a new perspective.

"There is a glory and heroic posture to cranberry-stained hands that most men will never experience," he bemoaned. "Not quite as out of reach as childbirth but, in our culture, pretty close."

According to Bill, if women are up to their elbows in cranberries and tinsel, it's all our own doing. Men would like to do more, but they're afraid.

"Much like oil tanker captains encountering a harbor pilot, guys know when to leave the bridge," he said. "And the smart ones either slip into their predefined specialties or stand by for orders."

Not knowing much about boats, I went to my husband for help.

"He means the holidays are like a storm coming," he said. "We just try to stay out of the way and not get covered with mess."

I felt so guilty. It's bad enough that men can't fully experience childbirth. It's a downright atrocity how we go and rob them of Christmas.

Take a look at the magazines. Women are running the show. Every fall, there's advice on how to simplify the holidays by making 100 gifts for less than $10 while losing 10 pounds a week.

And the advice is all from women. The same women who have anxiety attacks every November over the growing urge to make monogrammed chenille bathrobes for every adult member of the family. The same ones who spend every Christmas Eve decorating individual sweet potato casseroles with pecans.

Imagine how much simpler the holidays would be if we left them up to men.

No man I've ever known has worked himself into a sweat making 100 gifts for under $10. Or even one gift for under $10. And the last man reported to be bent over a chenille bathrobe on Christmas Eve was not sewing it.

For a sample of what men's holiday advice would be, I called up a few. I have to admit the suggestions were spectacularly efficient.

Jim invests maybe 30 minutes to come up with perfect holiday gifts for his wife.

"She goes to a favorite outlet store, tries on lots of stuff and has them put aside seven or eight outfits she likes," he said.

"They call me. I run over and pick out two or three, and I'm done. They fit! The color's right! The price is right! And she's surprised!"

One guy my friend Lora dated handled his entire shopping list with one trip to a 24-hour superstore, usually at midnight just before Christmas.

My neighbor Rich browses the Internet for ideas before he ever leaves home.

And my hairdresser Rita said her friend Bob accompanies his wife to the store as she holds up each gift for questioning.

"Right color? Right size? Would they use it?" he asks.

If the answer is yes, it's in the cart.

"It's up to us to buy it and up to them to like it," he said. With his help, the shopping's done in a couple of days.

Impressed by all of this, I told my daughter the other night that men are so efficient, I thought it was only right that we turn more of the holiday joy over to them — not just shopping but cooking and decorating and mailing out-of-town packages.

"Why?" she asked.

"Much like oil tanker captains encountering a harbor pilot, we women have to learn when to leave the bridge," I explained.

"Huh?" she said.

I gave it another try.

"Think of it as a gift," I told her. "Men don't get to experience childbirth, and we're about to make it up to them."

Stocking Stuffing Stress Still Stalks Me

As we plowed through the Wal-Mart parking lot the other day, fingers numb from the 600 pounds of gifts we'd crammed into two dozen plastic handle bags, my mom, then 83, took a moment to reflect on the good old days.

"When I was a girl, we just got fruit in our stockings," she said. "Just fruit. And those little free samples Aunt Rana sent away for all year. Little bottles of lotion and makeup. Life was simpler then."

I laughed at the time, trying to imagine how a sock full of grapefruit, tangerines and apples would be greeted at our house on Christmas morning. But half a tank of gas and a full headache later, I'm ready to make Aunt Rana the patron saint of stocking-stuffers.

In our house alone, estimating conservatively and using premium fruit, a grapefruit or two and a couple dozen apples and tangerines could save us at least 12 hours, three migraine headaches and a couple of hundred dollars a year.

I realize as soon as I say it that I know that not everyone will agree. I know — because they happily announce it — that some folks joyfully squirrel away stocking stuffers all year long and are completely prepared for the winter. Others have simply lowered their families' expectations. As they tell it, there is unbridled rejoicing at trial size bottles of Dial antibacterial soap and Head & Shoulders shampoo.

But for me the perfect has become, as they say, the enemy of the possible. Stufferless and stymied, I am still searching for the perfect seven or eight items per person. Each not too practical but not too useless. Each not too expensive but not too cheap. Each no bigger than a Band-Aid box but reflecting the recipient's personal interests and taste. Each purchased secretly while its recipient is waiting in the car.

I'm all finished except for the stockings. But in the school of Christmas shopping, I am like the Ph.D. candidate who hasn't started her dissertation. There's a long road ahead, and I need a couple of extensions.

This is not for lack of helpful suggestions from bystanders in the stocking race. Their advice each year breaks down into four major categories:

"Start early!" This counsel, rarely offered before mid-December, is as useful as telling a woman with six children hanging on her arm in the post office line that she probably should have mailed the packages to Taiwan before December 21.

"Think big!" It's true that each tall can of hairspray, slid down the center of a stocking, saves at least 60 minutes of shopping time. But for those who must personalize each gift, it takes another 30 to write a poem explaining it.

"Just buy gift certificates!" Not bad, as long as each one is packed in a container the size of a videotape. Otherwise, the average stocking holds approximately 3,624.

"Just buy toiletries!" This last, the hands-down winner with pre-teen girls, can now work for everyone, including the family dog. Exquisitely packaged lotions, creams and sprays with names like Zesty Grapefruit, Tangy Tangerine and Sparkling Green Apple are ready for the picking. Unless, of course, they don't smell exactly like Zesty Grapefruit, Tangy Tangerine and Sparkling Green Apple.

In which case, the only choice would be to go for the real thing.

Only One Wise Man Brought Gold

Ever on the lookout for time-savers, I was blown away when my friend Jean said she didn't do Christmas shopping for her adult children.

"I'm terrible," she said. "I just write a check."

"Not terrible!" I told her, feet still hurting from last year's hunt. "Money's what they want! Money's what they need! I've never seen one of them return it."

The prospect of a shopping strike left me reeling. Mentally, I fast-forwarded to two weeks before Christmas under a no-shopping plan. I am sitting in front of the fireplace, sipping red wine (for my health) and tucking three checks into gift envelopes to be hung from the tree. I have purchased lovely cards for my spouse and my mom. And I've gone to the Heifer International website (http://www.heifer.org) and notified my out-of-town relatives that a share of a water buffalo has been donated to a third-world country in their names.

The scene made lots of sense. "I have a way too complicated Christmas!" I shouted to my husband. "I spend hours shopping and wrapping and tagging, and it's all over in two minutes."

"All over but the returns," he said.

"I'm done with that!" I declared. "From now on, I'm doing it the easy way."

He needed no convincing. Jewish himself, he stopped participating in the gift craze the year I sent him to Toys "R" Us on Christmas Eve.

"This is something Christians invented to torture themselves," he said then. "Count me out." He was delighted at the thought I might join him.

"Absolutely," I said, throwing in a little Christian theology. "You go back to the very first Christmas, and one of the three wise men brought gold. If gold was good enough for Jesus, then cash should certainly work for the kids."

That was a month ago. Now I am embarrassed to report that as sensible as the whole approach seemed then, I have gotten only as far as the water buffalo.

"What's in those shopping bags?" he asked the other day.

"Oh, just a few things to wrap up for the kids," I said. "So it doesn't look so bare under the tree. Besides, I want to show that I'm still in tune with who they are, that I can still find the perfect gift."

"Really?" he said. I detected a slightly raised eyebrow.

"Don't even bring up the Western shirts I bought the boys," I said.

"No," he said. "I was thinking of the red platform shoes you bought our daughter."

The truth is, the best that can be said about my gift-giving history is that it's been memorable. It's not that I don't put a lot of thought into what goes under the tree. It's just that once inspiration strikes, like a moth to the flame, I cannot stop myself from pursuing the unique, no matter how ill-advised.

"Since you bring it up," he said, "the Western shirts were a little over the top."

"The boys both liked country music at the time," I pointed out. "Who knew they wouldn't want matching plaid shirts with pearl buttons from the JCPenney catalog?"

"There was a clue," he said. "They wore nothing but jeans and black turtlenecks at the time."

"What about the platform shoes?" I said. "Didn't they make sense? She's short, and they made her taller."

"She was very polite about not wanting them," he said. "Remember how she kept apologizing on the way back to the mall?"

"True. But at least they took them back without a fight."

As soon as I said that, I knew I was in trouble because my need to keep shopping is surpassed only by my need to confess.

"We weren't so lucky with the navy church hat I bought my mom," I said, going on to explain how the pricey monstrosity with the giant silver bow wound up in the Amvets box after the online hatmaker declined to take it back.

"Great Christmas pictures that year," I added. "Remember her surprise when she tried it on?"

It would seem, with so little success, that I would stop the craziness and simply write a check.

But instead, I gleefully continue to brainstorm, to Google for gift ideas, to make lists, to find "perfect gifts," and to subtract $10 here and $10 there from the amount we've budgeted.

"What would Christmas be without surprises?" I asked. "What would Christmas be without hope?"

It's not that I've rejected the simplicity of writing a check. Maybe I'm just following the lead of the other two wise men. Off they went, in search of the unique. And they came up with something way more far-fetched than red platform shoes or a Western shirt. They came up with dried tree sap, more glamorously referred to as frankincense and myrrh.

Come to think of it, not a bad idea. And — yes! — available online this year for only $69.95.

January Ushers in Queen of Clean

Help! I can't stop!

The New Year's confetti had barely hit the rug when the rampage started. Spring does it for some, but January turns me into the Quintessential Queen of Clean.

Enough of the tree that's dropped its needles! Enough of the dried gingerbread dough that clings to the kitchen floor!

At 12:01 a.m. and after four billion fallen pine needles, I'm ready to yank the twinkling lights that seemed so charming and pitch the whole triangular affair over the back deck rail.

"Time to get back to normal!" I shout, groping to remember what "normal" was. "Time to clean up and get organized!"

No one at our house yells "Hurray!"

Decorating and un-decorating are a lot like buying a family dog. Much excitement on the front end but little enthusiasm for the pooper-scooper.

Whisper "Anyone for pizza?" and you get "Yeah! Pepperoni!"

Yell "Time to take the tree down!" and everyone is vacationing in Missouri.

One year, I tried threats. "No home-cooked meals until this cleaning is done!" For reasons I have not explored, this had no effect.

Besides, with most unpleasantries, bribery works best. So this year, I tried the movie method.

"Movie starts at 2:10. It's 11:05. Everybody on it, and we'll be cleaned up and out the door by 2."

It worked. We stashed the ornaments in Ziploc bags, picked pine needles out from under the molding and tangle-proofed twinkle lights by wrapping them around our wrists and elbows. In the end, we threw the tree over the back deck rail till pick-up day and were sitting in the car, motor running, by 2.

But, I must confess, it didn't stop there for me.

Even after we sucked the last icicle into the vacuum (is there ever a last icicle?), ate a tub of popcorn and watched Mel Gibson read Helen Hunt's mind, I still needed cleaning comfort.

I needed the comfort that comes from clearing an entire shelf of towels and stacking them in those little same-size piles you find in hotel bathrooms. ("Just stay there. Don't move. And nobody touch!")

I needed the comfort that comes from alphabetizing an entire shelf of spices, the reassurance that comes from knowing that in an orderly, post-holiday world, cloves will always come before ginger, nutmeg before paprika.

It is this need of mine for order — not laziness on their part — that my family claims has made them shrink from this annual Clean Fest.

"Don't you think you're going a little overboard?" our daughter wanted to know the other night as we left the house in a snowstorm for a sale on closet organizers.

"They'll be sold out!" I explained, gripping the wheel.

But lucky for us, no competition. By midnight, we'd jammed 14 polyurethane treasures into the trunk, encased every last toiletry in a dust-proof dwelling and moved on to clear the kitchen shelves of superfluous cookbooks.

"Cookbook clearance!" I announced. "Who wants to keep *Quiches for Vegetable-Lovers?*"

Silence. Not a word.

I don't think it was a sign of disinterest. I suspect that at that moment they, too, had caught a glimpse of that little silver strand dancing naughtily on the heating vent.

Anyway, there was much hooting and hollering as I lunged across the kitchen to capture it.

I'm sure it was applause.

Leash Laws

Simplifying holidays. If you love the proverbial hustle and bustle but feel exhausted by New Year's Day, try limiting the frantic activities to only one of your frenetic favorites each year. You might limit yourself to one daylong shopping spree at the mall at the height of the season or one full day of cookie baking until your feet ache. But simplify the other activities. During the shopping spree year, you might purchase home-baked goods from a friend who's looking to make extra money. During a baking year, you might do your shopping online. That way, Frantic and the Simplifier will each get their way, and your life will be more in balance.

Sharing the joy. Since men seem less stressed over holiday preparations, it's time women let the men in their lives take over and do what they do best: procrastinate painlessly. Three requirements, though: clear instructions, no second-guessing and lavish praise. Sisters, is that too great a price to pay to reclaim a life when it's your own?

Stuffing those stockings. If you can't bring yourself to claim you totally forgot about stockings or decided to donate the money to a Haitian orphanage, then separate the Sock Hop from the rest of the season. The third week in July might be a good time to shop for stocking stuffers. Make a day of it, list your finds and, if you're a wrapper, roll each treasure in tissue paper and place it in a bag with the recipient's name on it. Just imagine, when everyone else is saying, "I've got it all done but the stocking stuffers," you can say, "Good job!" Or else your friends will hate you.

Writing a check. Unless it's for charity, I'm not a fan of writing a check to simplify holiday gift-giving. For one thing, it feels impersonal. For another, I'm not in a position to write a check that would make a tremendous difference in the recipient's lifestyle. A small gift that says, "I've been paying attention to what you're interested in" is more fulfilling to give and hopefully to receive. Just pay attention to what people are interested in!

Disaster-proofing the holidays. At the end of the season, it helps to list what went right and what went wrong. Then, tape it to the Christmas tree stand or cookie recipe book so you actually bump into it before the big day. Read it over before the next season begins. Then take precautionary measures.

Coming clean. There's a reason plastic organizing boxes are on sale in January. It's therapeutic to leave the holiday season with a clean sweep, de-cluttering all the extra stuff, all the bangles and pine needles and fake snow. A fresh new year is about to begin. Rush the season with a spring wreath on the front door.

Chapter Eight

Food Eats Time Like a Hungry Dog

According to Cousin Geraldine, her dog Jesse could open the refrigerator, help himself and close the door with his nose.

I don't know whether I believe this, but I do know that food shopping, cooking and clean-up eat up time every bit as fast as Jesse could sneak out a pot roast.

With a salute to the Italians, who praise "the process," I must confess I've turned to "processed" and "fast" and sometimes just a bowl of cereal.

Deliver Me from the Big Oven, Please

Its demise was poorly timed.

I had cleverly scooted out the door to run errands and left my daughter and mother up to their elbows in chilled cookie dough to roll and cut and bake. Sadly, I hadn't hit more than two stores before my pager went off.

First, it was the baker's apprentice. "Mom! There was a spark, then a lot of smoke. I had to shut the oven off!"

Then it was the Grand Baker herself: "I told you so."

She had. It came as no real surprise that after 25 years, our gold-enameled oven had finally exploded. There had been a few warnings, but I'd discounted each one as unimportant in my larger life.

The time-bake function had kicked in a full 12 hours early one day and turned a frozen chicken into charcoal. But with a small microwave, who really needs time-bake? Cookies had always burned on the bottom rack, but how often did we bake cookies? Cakes never rose very well, but how often did we bake cakes?

"Believe me, it works well enough for my needs," I had told my mother.

To which she had countered: "I simply don't understand how anyone can function without a working oven."

This statement came just an hour before the oven's dramatic end, while it was still barely working and she was calculating the time it would take to bake several pounds of dough one sheet at a time.

Rushing home to inspect the remains, I was nonchalant.

"It's probably just the heating element," I yawned.

But the discussion didn't end there. We embarked on the household debate that ensues with the death of every harvest gold major appliance in our '70s house. Should we keep repairing at substantial cost? Or, at exorbitant cost, should we go look for a replacement, only to make the inevitable discovery that the year ours was installed, the bottom quarter panel was one-quarter-inch shorter than standard?

Those who argued that the oven is 75 percent dead anyway, an unfashionable color and probably even dangerous won out.

The one person who argued that the relic could be salvaged well enough did not.

So it has been that for the last month and a half, we have not called a repairman and have not had a working oven. We are instead looking forward, eventually, to some sleek black "flat-top" model that will allow me to bake incredible delicacies never before possible and to cook large quantities of food for legions of dinner guests.

Anyone who has seen the commercials for these big ovens knows that they are frightening. Women once completely sane are now surrounded by huge quantities of gourmet food they are obsessed with making – whole turkeys and cherry pies and chocolate cakes and clove-studded hams and tuna noodle casseroles for 24 with hand-crushed crumb toppings.

The truth is that in the last month and a half, we have been operating ovenlessly and nicely in a minimalist sort of way. Bagels toast to perfection in the toaster oven. Meat chars itself neatly in a Lean Mean Fat Grilling Machine. And dinners in tiny boxes pirouette happily for nine to 12 minutes on a turntable.

As for dinner guests and meaningful contributions to potluck dinners, they have simply been postponed in favor of the day — someday and faraway — that our oven comes back.

The lesson in this has been unmistakable. I don't have a working oven, but compared to the TV Food Woman, I am saving hundreds of hours.

"Enjoy the break!" the Grand Baker advised with astonishing flourish the other day as the supplier, still searching for the right size, announced another delivery delay.

What does she think I was doing all along?

'Gourmet' All Comes Down to Garnish

Next summer, I'm raising nasturtiums. I'm convinced after a weekend at a country inn that nasturtiums might be the only thing standing between me and *Gourmet Magazine*.

"Wow!" said every guest, staring at a bright Fiestaware platter mounded with fresh melon, pineapple and grapes. "Look at those flowers!"

"You can eat them," offered the hostess, who had immediately disclosed herself as a naturalist by garnishing the salade nicoise with organically grown flowering garlic. I hadn't felt so exotic since I ate the orchids off the sherbet at a wedding.

"It's all in the presentation," whispered the woman in line behind me. "There's really nothing to it."

I think she has a point.

Look at any gourmet magazine. No recipe stands alone.

Take the beet carpaccio with goat cheese and mint vinaigrette touted in one magazine as a winner for an elegant brunch. On top of the soft fresh goat cheese, fresh shallots, walnut oil and a dozen other items we all keep around the house, we are to "sprinkle with chives." After removing the vanilla bean from which we have previously scraped the seeds, the lemon panna cotta with blackberry sauce requires a garnish of fresh mint and three blackberries. The smoked salmon benedict (a winner with kids everywhere) requires a "garnish of dill sprigs, if desired."

I might not have time to mince the shallots; whisk them with mustard, wine and cream; poach eggs one at a time in hot water; make cream sauce in a double boiler and transfer everything to toast triangles. But I bet I could manage to nestle a couple of dill sprigs and an orange slice just to the right of an Egg McMuffin.

The truth is that garnishing is what it's all about. Only innkeepers buy these magazines to cook from them. The rest of us buy them to put in the bathroom rack, the only place we have time to look at the pictures. But for 10 percent of the effort, we can get

90 percent of the effect.

Imagine a mold of Hamburger Helper encircled by three-quarters pound of plum tomatoes, halved and seeded, interspersed with sprigs of fresh rosemary. Or a hand-painted pasta bowl filled with steaming blue-box mac-and-cheese accented with mint sprigs and fresh cilantro.

Or even a salade nicoise.

"This doesn't look like it would be *that* hard to make," I announced to the innkeeper, who had just presented a platter glistening with herbed potatoes, beans and tuna. "Pretty much beans and potatoes with a few garnishes, huh? I bet you could make that ahead."

She blanched. "I'd be happy to share my recipe," she said.

It went on for only a single-spaced page but required peeling a half-inch band around the center of 24 small potatoes and trimming and cooking two pounds of beans, all just before serving, so that the homemade herbal dressing (eight ingredients) was absorbed to the max.

I did notice she placed it all on a bed of lettuce leaves and added a garnish of garlic flowers, tomatoes and olives.

The perfect setting, I think, for a drive-thru potato salad.

Cooking in Italia Cannot Be Rushed

It started innocently enough in the laundry room. The wall above the set tub was boringly blank.

'It needs something," I told my husband, "a piece of art."

"In the laundry room?" he said.

"I seem to spend a lot of time there."

As it turned out, I was only an arts festival away from finding just the thing — a quaint photograph of laundry hanging between two buildings that lined a narrow street. The street happened to be in Italy.

"A place I've always wanted to go!" I said each time I saw it.

By the 730th load, my family was ready — no, eager — for me to go there.

"Go while you still can," said my mom, in a worrisome reference to my age. "It will be my treat."

Some serious clicking on the Internet produced a boatload of Italian touring opportunities. Without elaborating on my culinary interest or abilities, let's just say everyone was pleased and astonished to learn I'd chosen cooking lessons in Tuscany, where food is known as an art, not a carryout meal.

The week-long itinerary was mind-blowing: three hands-on cooking lessons with Italian chefs on top of shopping and museum jaunts into Florence and demos by artisans making everything from olive oil to Gucci bags.

Once there, I'm not sure whether I was more astonished by Tuscany's postcard vistas at every turn or the fact that I went an entire week without a salad bag or a mini-peeled carrot.

I sensed that my fellow travelers from around the country — seven women and one share-the-cooking couple — had worked a bit harder at the chopping board than I before flying to Italy for further instructions. They asked probing questions.

"Could you use an immersion blender for that?" one

wanted to know.

"What is an immersion blender?" was my question.

But novice or master, each one of us was mesmerized by the passion and care with which our Italian chefs approached their cooking.

"The food must be fresh," said Vincenzo, breathing in handfuls of just-picked basil, "and you must take your time."

As he chopped and philosophized, it became clear that in Italy, it is the process of cooking, not simply the final product, that is valued. Like the air-dried laundry in the picture above our set tub, the process cannot be rushed.

In that spirit, our chef-instructor proceeded to defile food processors and half-cooked mushrooms in favor of working with a knife or mezzaluna and sautéing mushrooms until they were "golden." I tried to be unfazed by the fact that it was taking 10 of us two hours to chop, sauté, squeeze lovingly and crumble our way to cold bread salad and meat "purses" laced with a sauce of red wine, raisins and capers.

"Don't worry," said Vincenzo, "You can make it all ahead."

With that, there was a collective sigh of relief. Not that we would rush things, of course. But, as one southern hostess in our group pointed out, "We need time to visit with our guests." It was a display of wisdom that I would not fully appreciate until I got home.

Exactly when we would have time to make it all ahead did not come up in Italia. But mentally calculating on the trip home, I figured that between two and four on Wednesday morning looked promising for cooking, peeling and hollowing out potatoes, and filling them with mushroom parmesan béchamel sauce.

If I could freeze them, I figured I could substitute my Tuscan potatoes for the usual tater tot and canned mushroom soup recipe on our Christmas Eve buffet. But there was some dispute between the chef and our tour leader about whether freezing was advisable.

The question was still not resolved by the time I arrived

home with a wad of Tuscan recipes and to a husband who had issued dinner invitations to the entire neighborhood.

"They can't wait to see what you've learned!" he said.

"Well, I learned more about the process of cooking than the final product," I tried to explain. "The real joy is in drinking a little wine, doing a little chopping, taking all the time you need."

He seemed puzzled.

"If they really want to learn about Tuscan cooking, tell them to be here at three wearing aprons."

So he did. We ate around nine.

Serial Cooking's Out, Cereal's In

I was surprised to learn the other day that the fast-food breakthrough of the moment is no longer low carb, dough-less pizza. It's cereal.

College students in Arizona are giving rave reviews to a restaurant concept called Cereality, at which waiters clad in pajama tops serve them 33 choices of cereal with 34 choices of toppings in leak-proof containers flooded with milk.

"A dream come true!" claims one of these students on the company's Web site. "Since I was five, I wished I could have a different cereal every morning. Now I can have all of them at the same time too!"

Cereality fans predict the concept will sweep the nation, with milk-laden cocoa puffs and malted milk balls (which the menu calls "The Devil Made Me Do It") soaring above burgers and fries as the fast food of choice. And the implications for home cooking are boundless.

"I'll never have to cook again," I announced to the family the other night, after a glance into the pantry. "We have ingredients here for 33 meals!"

There was no denying it. Just on the bottom shelf, there were Lucky Charms, Shredded Wheat, six kinds of flavored oatmeal, raisins from last December and a 3-inch pouch of dark brown sugar with a twist-tie. An elbow-length reach into the boxes above produced enough circles, buds, flakes and shreds to mix countless combos that could be topped with leftover coconut, bananas, chocolate chips and marshmallows.

"How about a Chocolate Chip Coconut Shredded Bonanza for breakfast?" I offered. "Or an Oat-So-Good Mallo Rumba Rhymer for dinner?"

My husband groaned.

"How about a chicken dinner?" he asked. "How about grilled halibut and steamed vegetables?"

But I continued, undeterred. "Do you have any idea how

much guilt and money we could save if we actually finished off all this stuff?" I asked.

Reaching for the Eggbeaters and a skillet, he seemed unmoved, like a man unacquainted with the true Cereality of life, like one who had never felt the guilt of cleaning the pantry by cramming handfuls of honey oat granola grains down the disposal late at night.

The fact is that there's nothing less appealing than several inches of lifeless cereal snoozing at the bottom of what was once a $5 box of crunch. I did not grow up in the Depression, but the idea of reviving these sad particles on cookie sheets at 250 degrees or tossing them with a dash of Worcestershire and garlic salt has crossed my mind. And the thought of layering them in creative parfaits has me practically breathless.

"Think of all the time we'd save!" I pressed, envisioning the kitchen island set out like a self-service motel breakfast bar where frosty colored circles and pillows of dried wheat would sun themselves in goldfish bowls beside stacks of bagels in plastic sleeves.

"What about cooking?" he wanted to know.

"Fortunately, it would end."

Despite my best efforts, the idea of a Seinfeld-esque existence at home did not sell. And our daughter, then just a couple of years away from campus life, predicted it would be a sure-fire failure at other colleges and at airports where the pajama-topped waiters are headed next.

"When you go out for breakfast, you want breakfast," she explained. "Eggs. Pancakes. Bacon. Nobody goes out for a bowl of cereal. You can eat that all the time at home."

All the time. Yes! What an excellent idea.

Backyard Grill's
My Dirty Little Secret

A long time ago, I figured out that the only way to cook in the summer was to fire up the grill.

"Isn't that a lot of trouble?" my husband asks.

"Not if you're doing it," I say.

But the truth is that even if he's not, there's nothing easier than throwing some chicken breasts in a plastic bag after breakfast, dousing them with Italian dressing and tossing them onto the backyard inferno after work. Plopped on the contents of a salad bag and garnished with a strawberry, they're as dressy as a $12.99 dinner entrée at a patio restaurant.

The only question is whether the easier part of grilling is the cooking or the clean-up.

"With grilling," I pointed out the other day, "there's no clean-up at all. And there's no limit to what you can do. I overheard a woman at the grocery store who makes pizza on the grill. How easy is that?"

The moment I said it, I knew I was in trouble.

"What do you mean 'no clean-up'?" our daughter asked.

Ever since she took a Family Consumer Science class in middle school, my germicide-ability has been questioned

"Do you know," she'll say, "that a sponge is the filthiest thing in the kitchen? Don't ever wipe the counter with a sponge."

"Did you touch raw meat?" she's apt to say, noticing eight hamburger patties laid out to be grilled.

"No, they simply appeared."

Guiltily, I head off more questions by professing to have washed my hands the absolute instant I made the last patty in total compliance with the safe-handling instructions on the package.

She gives me a look. It says, "I'm lucky to be alive." Which explains why I should never have raised the subject of grilling.

"What do you mean there's no clean-up?" she asked.

"Well, I scrape it off with a brush, fire it up and kill the germs."

"That's it?" she said.

"That's all anybody does." An unofficial poll of my busiest and most laid-back friends confirmed the truth of this statement.

"Some people only use a wad of aluminum foil instead of a brush," I informed her. "Liz, for example, can't believe anyone would do more than fire up and scrape." I didn't mention that Liz had also confessed to using bacon and Tylenol way beyond the expiration dates.

I also didn't mention how my friend Linda's grill looked this spring after it was packed away for the winter with barbecued chicken pieces still on it. Or how she redeemed it in seconds by simply firing up and scraping.

I did disclose that an Internet search turned up a guy in South Carolina who cleans his grill at the beach by kicking sand on it and rubbing it with the soles of his shoes. This was to show the bizarre ways in which grill-cleaners behave.

"Gross!" I exclaimed impressively. "Imagine the grit!"

I also mentioned the red-letter warning that appears on bottles of grill cleaner.

"How can something that can't touch your children, your eyes or your skin be safe to put on your grill?" I asked.

I was making progress, and I believe I would have completely won the grilling-cleaning wars if I hadn't mentioned the pizza. The thought of throwing a round of well-oiled dough on blackened char bars even made me queasy. But oddly enough, she seemed willing to try it.

"Could be good," she said, "but the grill would have to be like new."

"New?"

"You would need to scour it completely with antibacterial soap and water, then put it in the dishwasher and rinse it off really well to do pizza," she said.

Even I had to agree that the thought of white dough picking up charcoal bits was too revolting.

"Are we having the pizza soon?" she asked, almost too hopefully.

"It may take years," I said. "But I promise. It will be the first thing we make on our next new grill."

Leash Laws

Simple meals. Even if your oven's working, you can pretend you don't have one. Call it being environmentally responsible. If you rely exclusively on the toaster oven and microwave, you'll save lots of energy and simplicity is almost guaranteed. A baked potato, frozen entrée and a salad. How much time can that take?

School snacks. With food allergies on the rise, some school districts are banning snacks brought from home. If at all possible, move into one of these districts. It will save you a lot of time. If you cannot move, then bring only store-bought snacks with the ingredient label intact on the pretext that it will be easier to check for allergens. Tell them that, otherwise, you would have baked from scratch.

Garnishes. Just say yes to them. A few basil leaves, some sprigs of fresh rosemary, and you'll look like you know how to identify a few basil leaves and some sprigs of fresh rosemary. If you don't, just be sure it's not poison ivy.

Not-so-fast food. Invite an army of friends over if you want to prepare a slow-cooked meal that requires a lot of dicing and chopping. Even better, have them bring some of the ingredients you'll be chopping and dicing. Bill the evening as a gourmet cooking experience for which chefs charge $69.95 a head, plus wine. Your new name is Tom Sawyer.

Serial cooking. Or was that *cereal*? Breakfast for dinner could have a whole new meaning if the ever-popular self-service cereal breakfast could pass for dinner at least once a week. A real food pyramid builder: grains, dairy and fruit. With a bowl of salad topped with tuna or chicken for lunch, yay! If you built any more pyramids, you'd be an Egyptian.

Drive-thru meals. Even with the healthier versions that have been concocted since the publication of *Fast Food Nation*, your best bet is a cooler full of apples, arugula and other fruits and veggies. In case you've ever indulged in a fast food salad and saved the plate, it fits right on top in a cooler. Good health and recycling all in one!

Grilling. Non-stick aluminum foil is my nominee for most "likely to cause a clear conscience about grill cleaning." Poke some holes in it so the smoke still comes through, and you're all set. Even food that normally burns onto the grill will lift off this stuff. It will still taste way too dry if you overcook it, but that's what barbecue sauce is for.

Chapter Nine

When Retail Is Not Therapy

Not all shopping is created equal. It's one thing to spend an afternoon examining the latest power tools or power shoes, quite another to push a cart through the grocery and compare the prices of organic and non-organic fat-free milk.

Too many choices, too many errands, too many returns. It's enough some days to make a person check out.

From Clueless to Wireless

Cleaning out the basement the other day, I ran into a pack of those old preprinted grocery lists, the long skinny ones that listed "the basics," like toothpaste and lettuce, ice cream and macaroni.

I tossed it.

"Don't throw that away!" said my mom, diving into the trash. "It's perfectly good. And a timesaver! Everyone in the family just checks off what they need. No more list-making"

"Ah!" I said, pretending to savor an extra 45 minutes a week. "I'll have to give that a try."

I hated to confess, but if I shopped from a list that said "toothpaste," I'd need to bring a sleeping bag. A trip just through the frozen food section would eat my prime time local calling minutes for a month.

Maybe everyone else can remember whether the tube on the bathroom counter says "Sparkling white with tartar control" or "Sparkling white without tartar control" or "Sparkling white with baking soda and peroxide." But I can't.

As it is, there are so many choices that there's no such thing as a quick trip to the store. Every visit is mind-boggling.

I struggle not just to bring home the bacon but to stand over the meat case and debate between applewood-smoked or maple-cured, microwave-ready or ready-to-eat, hardwood-smoked or country-peppered.

Even with a handwritten list, I'm clueless and forced to go wireless.

"What do you mean 'Old Spice CO?'" I yell into the cell. "Classic original," my husband screams back, voice crackling among 57 kinds of deodorant on the far aisle.

It's no better with once-upon-a-timesaver salad bags. There are now 19 different possibilities — everything from baby organic spring mix to classic American to classic mostly-brown-around-the-edges American. I call again.

"What's 'C salad'?" I want to know, a bag in each hand.

"Chicken," he says, directing me to the deli. "Tuna would be a T."

Mac-and-cheese is no better. There are more than 20 unfrozen possibilities —spirals and SpongeBob heads, pizza-flavored, nacho cheese, white cheddar, something called "extreme cheese" and a kit that lets you bake chicken on top. I call again.

"Which one?"

"There's only one," I'm told. "In the dark blue box."

Moose tracks vs. safari tracks warrants a call from the ice cream case, but tomatoes are hardly worth checking. Who would care whether they are sauced, pureed, diced, crushed, stewed or chopped? Or diced Italian? Or with balsamic vinegar, basil and olive oil? (As opposed to green, peppered with onion and zesty mild chiles).

And after awhile, whether the shampoo and matching conditioner are strawberry, green apple, raspberry, aloe vera, lavender, chamomile, tropical coconut or fresia (a flower I've never actually seen nor picked) seems like a decision for the person who drove to the store.

I'm only out the same day because these days we don't have a small child or own a dog. No sweat for me about whether to buy no-tears anemone apple shampoo or go for the bubble gum, tropical punch, wild watermelon or go-go grape. No long pauses over whether the bottom will be covered with Cruisers, Swaddlers, Easy Ups or Drypers. And no need to wonder whether an overweight old dog should eat the turkey-flavored weight management chow or a mix for "seniors 7 and up."

The dog aisle isn't bad, though. Apart from the organic section and its one-of-a-kind ginseng juice, it offers the only store items available in just one choice. Doggie ice cream doesn't come in chunky monkey or peaches-n-cream. It just comes in, well, doggie, and doggie toothpaste just comes in beef, which means that the dog-lover market might be ready for a time-saving, preprinted list.

For the pooch who eats lettuce and mac-and-cheese, I have just the thing.

Speed Shopping Gives Time to Chill Out

OK, I admit it. I'm a winter-hater. Who has time to suit up for sub-zero chills or the organizational skills to find 16 layers to suit up at all?

But the lady I met at the grocery store last week had a point.

"I love winter!" she said. "My car is a second refrigerator!"

She was standing at the end of the checkout lane — spike heels, camel suit, gold jewelry checking her watch and bagging her groceries.

"Gotta watch my lunch hour," she explained.

There is nothing like finding a role model in the working world, someone who has apparently figured out how to get it all done before the weekend, then sit back and pretend she has a full-time maid. I'd been searching for such a woman, and there she was in my own town straddling the end of a checkout lane.

"Let *me* do this," she'd begged the clerk with a voice unwilling to wait for a bagger. One by one she fired cans of green beans and tuna into waiting plastic handle bags and knotted the ends.

"More secure for the ride," she said and then barreled through the icy lot at record speed.

This is not to say that speed shopping at lunch is something new. Who has not dined and darted for a birthday card from the 75 percent-off rack at the mall?

But lunching on a cheese sandwich left at 7:30 a.m. to chill on the passenger side and dashing to a nearby food mart with a well-made grocery list (items possibly arranged in aisle order) raises the sport to a daunting art form. Inspired by the lady in the camel suit, I decided to give it a try.

Calculating the walk to the car, the drive to the store, the wait at the checkout, the bagging, the loading, the drive back to work and the return — at a dead heat — to my desk, I could see I'd have only 27 minutes of prime shopping time.

"I can absolutely do this," I told my husband as I described the dashing dame. "But I need your list by 7 a.m. Thursday. And it has to be precise. No time for cell phone calls."

"And," I warned our daughter, "this has to be it. No running back for some bottle of Ice Blue Gatorade that you left off the list."

Wisely, they did not reply.

Lured by the vision of arriving home Friday, pantry fully stocked and some three-for-$10 bouquet blooming in the foyer, I undertook The Preparation Phase on Wednesday night.

After consolidating six jars of single Kosher dill spears into one, wiping grenadine syrup off three icy shelves and enduring the indescribable sound of globbing ketchup bottle to bottle, I wrote out a list and posted a menu on the refrigerator door.

"Wish me luck!" I called from the driveway the next morning, cheese sandwich at the ready, and worked furiously all morning toward a timely lunchtime escape. After that, it was a blur. Bread, green beans, a mixed bouquet — one by one they flew into the cart, into the bags and finally into the four-wheeled fridge outside in 25 minutes flat. So brilliant and speedy was the mission that an obviously admiring store clerk followed me breathlessly to the parking lot.

"She wanted my autograph!" I explained to my family as we unpacked the whole load that night.

The fact that I forgot to sign the credit card slip seemed hardly worth mentioning.

Confessions of an Errant Errand-Runner

Life would go better if I could leave the house list in hand and run my errands the way the how-to books say.

"Plot your course," the experts tell us, "and knock those errands out one by one."

The idea is No Backtracking, no "wish-I'd-stopped-at-the-cleaners" sighs.

All that's needed, they say, is a list of errands to be run in some logical order, prepared thoughtfully over morning coffee. That, and a back-seat errand box stacked with pick-up slips, returns and protein snacks in case of traffic.

"Then," they say, "you head for the car, and you're on your way."

Sadly, I get only as far as the errand box, a Ziploc bag of cashews and the end of our street.

"Back already?" my husband asked the third time the garage door went up. "I thought you just left."

I have. Several times. The truth is that streamlined errand-running works only for those capable of leaving a house just once. I have never, ever left the house only once. Two, three times I return.

At first, he suspected I was one of those obsessive-compulsive types who returns again and again to check the stove.

"I am not OCD," I insisted, and proved it one afternoon by leaving the stove flaming for several hours.

"On those rare occasions I have checked," I confessed at the time, "it has actually been on."

The truth, I explained, is that I've always done my best thinking in the car. In law school, I aced every exam on the drive home. After work, I brilliantly recreated my every conversation on the commute. It only makes sense that at home, I have honed my errand-running to an art form only behind the wheel.

"Dry cleaners first," I say. "But wait! It's right by the grocery. Better run back and check the chili recipe. Might be out of tomatoes."

Recipe in hand, I leave again, only to remember that the grocery also sells shelf paper.

"Nine inches wide or twelve?" I wonder, heading back for a tape measure, but I forget to add tomatoes to the list.

I wish we lived on a longer street in a larger neighborhood. Then I could vary my route back and my many happy returns might go unnoticed. Instead, we live in a circle around a park where neighbors tend to wave to passing traffic.

"Didn't we just wave to her?" they must think. "How many times today?"

My mood is not improved by being married to a one-trip man. He leaves once and comes back once with his handle-sack reliably full of whatever he set out for.

"It's easy," he says, and I envy him for a moment.

But then I remind myself that he is earning his A+ only in Errand-Running 101, not my accelerated graduate course in multiple errands. His self-described mission is to fetch a tub of cream cheese, not to empty an entire errand box.

"Ha!" I think. "I'd like to see *him* negotiate the dry cleaners, grocery, library, video store …."

I laugh uncontrollably at the frenzied picture, all the way back to buy the tomatoes.

The Perspiration of Expiration

It's hard enough to remember birthdays and dental appointments. But with the spring sports schedule and then the end-of-school finale, it's time to plan ahead — and something's got to go.

I vote for the tiny retail punch cards and stamp cards that are hiding in my purse.

Such a relief it would be to know they were gone! Then, there would be no chance that with a better memory and a more spectacular filing system, I could somehow punch my way to a free loaf of bread or stamp my way to free coffee.

Instead, they scowl at me and hide, refusing to be found while the thrift store clerk, smiling sweetly, makes the usual inquiries.

"Do you have one of our …? It looks like …, " and she holds up a sample.

It does not help at that moment to be a child of parents raised during the Depression. In the frantic pawing that follows, I unearth enough bargain-hunting credentials to fill the curriculum vita of a tenured professor. Not only are there little plastic swipe cards, but also special memberships in the car wash club, the ground coffee club, the gourmet coffee club, the shoe club, the Capitol Club (so I don't miss those savings at the Statehouse gift shop), plus an assortment of non-punch deals which will qualify me to receive 26 bagels if I appear on a Thursday and buy at least a dozen.

"I'm sure it's here somewhere!" I cry, trying to get one punch closer to a free bag of hotdog buns. The lady behind me shuffles her feet.

Still, in their favor, punch cards rarely expire. Maybe a better idea would be to lose the clunky metal file with 27 alphabetized categories of cents-off coupons that flies open with each sudden stop, papering the back seat of the car.

It is this little scrap collection of "Bags/Wrap" to "Soup" that presents the real challenges: to remember when they expire and then to decide what to do about it.

A coupon paging system might work — something that goes off in meetings, one beep for an ordinary redemption day, two for double coupons.

"Excuse me, but I have to go buy three boxes of pop-up tissues with aloe before midnight."

This could avoid expiration, which is important. Supermarket cashiers are second only to librarians in their ability to announce clearly when a due date has passed.

"June 15, 1998, on the cake mix – a record!" said one just last Saturday to a familiar person with a clunky metal coupon file.

But even when the date is still ahead and in this decade, the questions are still too perplexing to solve on the run.

There is absolutely not enough time between the end of the soccer game and the beginning of the track meet to decide whether it's worth buying two boxes of "Great-New-Chocolate-Flavor!" cereal by a major manufacturer to get the $1 off. Maybe not, considering everyone at home really prefers blueberry banana marshmallow granola made by somebody else.

And the 20-minute grocery run that's possible during a 30-minute piano lesson doesn't leave time to read whether using the 55-cent potato chip coupon means automatic entry in the "$25 Million Drawing!" or whether some greasy little card has to be fished out from the bottom of the bag and mailed in.

This is to say nothing of the challenge of keeping track of those quick-moving expiration dates on the six cups of yogurt that just landed in the cart for the price of three.

Another job for the meeting-time pager?

"Excuse me. Yogurt break. Who wants their fruit on the bottom?"

This Penny-Pincher's an Organic Cheater

I'd like to say I sleep only on organic cotton after enjoying a sip of hot organic herb tea.

I'd like to say the tea follows the all-natural, no-hormones-added chicken breast with brown rice that passes for dinner.

I'd like to say I always choose the pricier, homelier organic plums over their juicy conventional siblings in the next bin.

But the truth is, I'm an organic cheater.

"Were these sprayed with pesticides?" quizzes our daughter, home from college for the weekend. She inspects a fruit basket that in simpler times would have wowed a nutritionist: apples in three varieties, plums and nectarines.

"Only some," I confess, suddenly noticing I failed to peel off the non-organic labels.

"Only a couple," I confess again.

Three minutes in the door, and I have already disappointed this promising new member of the school sustainability club.

"Organics are better for you and for the environment," she points out.

"And they taste better, too," her dad chimes in.

Penny-pincher to the end, I've tried to prove them wrong. I've gone so far as to conduct blind taste tests reminiscent of the days when generic corn flakes first premiered at half the cost.

Back then, I'd switched the contents of the plain white box that had CORN FLAKES in large black letters with the box that had a script red K in the corner and waited for the nonreaction.

I was always disappointed.

"What *is* this stuff?" my husband would ask at the first taste of generic in disguise.

Passing off bulk fruit as organic works no better.

"This pear has no taste," he says. "Where is the little organic sticker?"

I started to say organic pears were not in stock, but there

was no point in that. Our local supermarket boasts a daily count of the number of organics available, and recently it's been in the triple digits. Actually, that's part of my problem.

Somehow, I trusted organic fruit more when it was available only from co-ops run by aging hippies with gray ponytails. I was more convinced I was saving the environment when the organic apples were showcased alongside barrels of millet and spelt, not by the Twinkies in my neighborhood chain store.

The other day, I finally spewed out my suspicions. "What if we're being suckered?" I asked. "What if these labels mean nothing? What if there's really a giant conspiracy to pass off regular food as organic? Did you ever think it might still be full of chemicals and hormones and antibiotics, and we're paying twice as much for it?"

Suffice it to say, the organic conspiracy theory did not fly at our house, and I've had to resort to other means to fit organics in our budget. Guilt, for example.

"Buy only what you can eat," I preach. "For the cost of a couple organic apples, you could feed a child in a third-world country for a week."

"Pick out the raspberries that don't have fuzz on them yet. They're worth $1.98 apiece."

But the best strategy for trimming organic food costs came straight from an article about sustainability that I found lying around the house.

In addition to explaining how to read produce label codes (a four-digit label is not organic; a label that begins with the number nine is), the article pointed out that it's more ethical to buy a locally grown conventional apple than an organic one flown in from New Zealand. Why? Because of the pollution caused by flying the organic one halfway across the world.

At last there's an answer to the fruit bowl question.

I can hardly wait for someone to hold up an apple and squint.

"Is it organic?" this person will say.

"No," I will reply. "Local, ethical and 79 cents a pound. Everything else was from New Zealand."

Few Happy Returns

"How lovely!" my mom said, pointing to the never-opened carton propped up against the Amvets box at the shopping center.

"Someone went and donated a brand new plant stand to charity!"

"Uh, people are just more and more generous," I said.

I hated to disillusion her, but the real story behind the box was not so hard to imagine. Truth be told, it had probably been knocking around in the trunk of someone's car for months on an extended ride to a customer service desk.

"What's that noise?" friends of some young family member had probably asked as the thing crashed and thumped every afternoon on the way home from some school's athletics field.

"Oh, it's just mom's plant stand," the young family member had probably replied, rolling her eyes. "She can never get around to returning anything." Returning would have had a heavy emphasis on the second syllable, with the "rrrr ...," stretched way out to roll with the eyes. It would have been uttered by one who in her own adult life would never forget a plant stand in the trunk of the car.

"Well, anyway," my mom continued, "I think it's nice that they did that, whoever it was."

"Yes," I agreed, failing to share with this frugal woman who raised me any references to the many happy returns I myself have never had. I failed, for example, to discuss the extreme challenge of gathering in one place the receipt for the AAAA batteries — and the item they would not fit into — and the AAAA batteries themselves. I didn't mention the impossibility of getting them back to the electronics store, which is around the corner from the grocery store where I shop every week.

I failed to mention that taped-on receipts usually get yellow and brittle and rip in two when they've been in the car trunk too long, and that customer service clerks are not so friendly when the item is returned after a 10-month rear ride.

I didn't mention the problem of no receipt at all, which brings on the ethical dilemma of choosing whether to fess up or to claim that the six cans of rust-resistant wild berry spray paint were actually a "gift." And I didn't mention the dilemma of no store at all because the plant stand purveyor shut its doors 10 months after the sale but before its customer made it through them again.

I didn't mention the possibility that the customer made it all the way to the customer service desk, but her head and her feet hurt while others explained why never-used toys were oozing battery acid. Or that during the wait, she started weighing the value of a tax deduction versus the value of a lowest-selling-price store credit that could be used only in the small home accessories section.

And I completely left out the hassle of mail order returns — the struggle to get to the post office in the first place and then standing in line to return ill-fitting mail-order bras and shoes.

She would probably have asked, "Why in the world would anyone order something like that through the mail, without trying them on?"

And I could have answered only, "To save time," which in the context of the conversation didn't seem like a very good answer.

So it was better just to stay with the happy conclusion that this was a particularly generous donor, this person who had dropped off the plant stand.

And that is mostly true. There was nothing wrong with it, really. The fact is, I just changed offices before I had time to put it together.

Leash Laws

Cell phone shopping. Try this ground rule, borrowed from a friend's pre-school: *You get what you get, and you don't throw a fit.* When it comes to shopping and most anything else, extreme people-pleasing is a sure formula for a high-maintenance family. Unless you want to live in one, turn your cell phone off while shopping.

Speed shopping. Buying groceries at lunchtime works so well in winter that it's almost worth changing jobs for one with convenient parking also located near a retail center. In the summer, don't lose heart. You can still run for those paper products at lunch and enjoy a farmers market and free samples early on Saturday morning.

Errand-running. The usual advice, to "plan your route," is absolutely correct. But it doesn't go far enough. Plan your route and each item you'll need to execute the errands on it. That's a winning M-O.

Coupon-chasing. Figure out before you clip what you'll actually use. If you can get 20 cents off a name brand but know the store brand will be less regardless, no point in clipping it. If the coupons are for processed foods that you rarely eat, don't bother. Once the coupons are down to a manageable pile, keep them in an organizer that's always in the car so they're always with you when you're out. And even better, you can review expiration dates and trash the unused ones when you have "found time." My favorite time for reviewing coupons is a trip through the carwash.

Shopping that's green and/or ethical and/or humane. Personally, I'd prefer to eat fairly priced food from humane local farmers who don't use chemical fertilizers or add hormones. That's what I prefer. Since I'd probably starve holding out for all my druthers, I've figured out a personal value system for food shopping and stick to it as closely as possible. Good resources for forming an opinion include Michael Pollan's book *The Omnivore's Dilemma: A Natural History of Four Meals* and Barbara Kingsolver's *Animal, Vegetable and Miracle*.

Returning merchandise, or not. Unless the item's a budget-breaker, don't beat yourself up over unreturned items unless you also fail to donate them to charity. This is particularly true if you're too busy to stand in the return line because you're working so many hours. Your act of charity can assist both you and a person who's less fortunate or not well enough to have an adequate source of income. A double bonus.

Chapter Ten

Bright Ideas, or Possibly Not

According to a refrigerator magnet my older son gave me, Albert Einstein once implored, "Out of clutter, find simplicity. From discord, find harmony. In the middle of difficulty lies opportunity."

Maybe because I am so frequently at the refrigerator, I've gone out of my way to follow Einstein's orders. True to his words, I have set out to set up systems that I believe will bring order out of chaos.

Not always with his genius.

The La De Da's of Cheating

My friend Lora spotted the mass of papers peeking out from under a couple of orderly looking scrapbooks.

"Oh!" she said. "You cheater-cleaned for us."

"Cheater-cleaned?"

"You know, running around, stacking things and throwing them in closets. What you do before company."

"Well, a little," I confessed, but I didn't let loose with the whole story.

Cheater cleaning, a.k.a. fast cleaning, has been a guilty closet secret of mine for years. If it weren't for the dinner party we had in 1996, my husband would still have the jacket to his brown wool suit.

"If you left it on the back of the recliner, then it probably went out to the garage in a garbage bag," I'm still explaining, "along with my ankle weights and that day's mail. You just don't leave things around when company's coming."

Since then, in my zeal to recreate the pages of *Southern Living* before the doorbell rings, we've lost a Walkman (make-your-own-sundaes party, 1998), a pair of new athletic shoes (Thanksgiving with Cleveland guests, 1999), the bottom half of a teal-and-black wind suit (Christmas dinner, 2001) and the receiver to a cordless telephone (neighborhood picnic, two Julys ago).

My mother says this is contrary to my childhood training.

"If you just picked things up at the end of every day," she's still insisting, "you would not have to go on these last-minute cleaning sprees."

Tall talking, I think, from someone who in the '50s was fast-cleaning the powder room faucets with rubbing alcohol and doing something called "la de da" cooking for my dad.

"If you get home late," she then told me, "just throw on your apron, comb your hair, switch on the stove, sauté some onions and say, 'La de da! Dinner's ready!'"

If she was also la-de-da vacuuming the carpets, she didn't let on. But long before Swiffers and disposable dust rags, a wise older woman at work had already tipped me off to that. She said I'd save hours if I just did "middles."

"It's what cleaning crews do," she explained. "Running the sweeper through the middle of the room making carpet marks. Looks like you've cleaned but only takes minutes!"

I told Lora about this. Impressive, she said, but not as clever as the new "bag method" of drawer cleaning.

"You don't mean emptying it all in a Ziploc and hiding it in the basement?" I asked.

"Exactly."

I was stunned that others were also sifting through used Chapsticks and broken pencils and twist ties in the kitchen junk drawer and finally dumping it all by handfuls in see-through bags. It was troubling to learn this original technique might not be as original as I'd thought.

"You have to keep the bag for several months," I cautioned, "to be sure there was nothing important in there, like jewelry."

"I know," she said.

I felt as deflated as Thomas Edison discovering that someone else had invented the light bulb.

"Bet it hasn't occurred to you why they're marketing those new Ziploc bags in 1x and 2x sizes," I pointed out.

She blinked.

"It's not just for storing sleeping bags, is it?"

I didn't confess. But the coat closet has never looked better.

There's Comfort in Finding the Nutmeg

It seems these days that there is no good news. We are in the midst of all-out war. Unemployment is up. The stock market is anybody's guess.

It would be nice in times like these to know absolutely what is right. To wave flags or write peace poems. To buy, sell or sit on what we have. To know which e-mails to forward and which icons to click to show support.

I would like to say I am sure, that I have signed up and waved or marched somewhere. Or that in an enlightened moment, I have written words or music so moving that others can find their way.

But this is not the case. And the real truth is that while others have gathered and marched and proclaimed, I am simply mulling it over and finding solace in a small corner of my kitchen cabinet.

I knew it would be like this when I spotted the large shiny boxes on a sale shelf at the grocery superstore. Orderly revolving teakwood canisters, each designed to hold 12 herbs and spices. In perfectly uniform jars. In alphabetical order.

There is something compelling about creating order in a world that seems to be falling apart, so buying three revolving spice racks on sale for $13.99 apiece, dumping the duplicate spices and washing the jars out, and creating little uniform labels that could be laminated and alphabetized suddenly made a great deal of sense.

The find followed several weeks of frustration when the disorder of the cabinet, like the disorder of the world, had seemed to come to a head. Marjoram was never where marjoram was supposed to be. The nutmeg was hiding behind a huge tin of Hungarian paprika. And the basil I couldn't find one day appeared in three different jars the next. Each pot of soup, each casserole seemed to result in a frantic search, an odd, over-the-top explosion, and finally a kitchen-chair climb to examine every single jar.

"Life will be much easier," I told my daughter, "if we don't have to keep looking for the nutmeg."

She seemed unconvinced.

But over the next few days, the project proceeded with a compulsion that placed it over all other priorities. As the headlines screamed "Tensions High!" I tossed grungy plastic turntables. Spread the contents of the cabinet onto the kitchen table. Shook cans of chili powder and ground mustard. Scorned duplicates. Checked for freshness. Emptied spice jars. Filled spice jars. Trashed a 12-year-old packet of saffron from a long-ago cooking class. Meticulously hand-cut computer labels and positioned them on jar lids.

As the news blares on, it is to this kitchen cabinet that I keep returning, opening and peering in, enjoying a reassuring peek.

It is good to be in a space where allspice always comes before bay leaves. Cumin always before dill weed. Fennel miles ahead of nutmeg.

A place with three spinning teakwood racks perfectly balanced and spinning nicely, not a squeak. Fragrances waiting to be tossed into squash or vegetable soup or apple pie.

Simon and Garfunkel would be proud, I think, remembering some lyrics from a simpler time.

Are you going to Scarborough Fair? Parsley, sage, rosemary, and thyme ....

Parsley, rosemary, sage and thyme, actually.

Simon and Garfunkel made great music. I suspect they were lousy at finding the nutmeg.

Poor Memory? Let's Celebrate

Blame it on my Palm, the one that blew out and sent my calendar entries into cyberspace.

Or blame it on my chaotic life.

Or blame it on my mind, the one our daughter's sure I've been losing since she turned 13.

Whatever the reason, I've developed birthday amnesia. Although I hate to admit it, I rarely remember a birthday beyond the immediate family.

This is particularly embarrassing because my own birthday — Valentine's Day — seems to be remembered by even the most casual acquaintances.

"Happy birthday," says the lady at the dry cleaners. And the postman. And my daughter's room mother from third grade.

Instead, I compliment a friend on her new necklace and blush when she says, "Thank you. I got it for my birthday last week."

On those rare occasions when I remember the month a friend was born, I try to send a card the very first week.

"What an early bird you are!" they'll exclaim.

Or "Thanks for the card. I love to keep the celebration going!"

If they happen to tell me it arrived right on time, I estimate the likely date and write it down, usually on a scrap of paper that takes an express ride to the recycling bin.

Oddly enough, I do remember one friend's birthday, so I went ahead and told her about the problem.

"You should subscribe to one of those virtual reminder services," she told me. "Most of them are free, and they'll even supply the card."

"That's great," I said, "if I knew the dates."

Being a resourceful sort, she came up with one that offers to send e-mails to all your friends asking for their birthdays.

"Isn't that a little weird?" I asked, "having some third party ask for me? They probably wouldn't even say how embarrassed I am. They wouldn't make up a credible excuse, like my PDA blew out or was stolen from the trunk of my car. And it's kind of creepy, like maybe next they'll be asking for a social security number."

My husband was no more help.

"Why don't you just ask people?" he wanted to know.

A one-time journalist, he has the chutzpah to ask anyone just about anything. I get that. When you've asked someone, "So you embezzled about $4.5 million?" in hopes of getting them to admit they took $100 grand, nothing seems audacious.

But it seemed awkward to me, particularly because — which I did not happen to tell him — I had asked some of my friends for this information before.

Finally, it dawned on me. Just as libraries designate fine-free days where they pardon us for overdue books, it's high time somebody declared an official Birthday Amnesty Day (BAD, for short), which everyone is encouraged to celebrate by gathering as many birthdays as possible.

"Ask Me About BAD" the T-shirts could say, "or 'BAD to the Bone.'"

There could even be chain e-mails set up to collect birthdays and prizes for those who gather the most.

I've got to think that Hallmark would get behind it, and American Greetings and all those Internet services that want us to buy annual subscriptions.

In the meantime, in case BAD takes awhile to take off, let me just say this to each of you:

Happy Birthday!

Overweight?
This Plan's a Sleeper

Thank God for researchers. Until a month or so ago, I thought every pound I gained could be traced to the cheese crackers that keep me going till dinner's on the table.

I was afraid that the occasional glass of wine along with the cheese crackers would add inches to my waist.

I even imagined that the recently idling recumbent exercise bike in our basement could put me on the road to obesity.

But now I know the truth. When I gain weight, it has nothing to do with food or exercise. It's simply because I'm not getting enough sleep.

According to a study presented at the American Thoracic Society International Conference in May 2006, women who sleep five hours per night are 32 percent more likely to experience major weight gain and 15 percent more likely to become obese than women who sleep seven hours.

I rushed home to share the news with the family.

"All I need to do to lose weight is sleep more!" I announced. "A study of middle-aged women proves it."

They were skeptical.

"Hate to say this," our daughter jumped in, "but maybe these sleepers lost weight because they stopped staying up eating ice cream in front of the TV."

"Not so," I replied. "It says right here that the women who slept less were actually eating less than the ones who got enough sleep. And they found no differences in the level of their physical activity. Weight loss is all about sleeping. Seven hours at a minimum."

Even though I found this hard to fathom, I forged ahead to develop a revolutionary new personal weight loss program that would work on these principles.

"The first step," I explained, "is figuring out where my time goes after work and why I'm not in bed by 10 p.m."

"I know," my husband said. "You're upstairs sending e-mail."

"Wrong."

"You're talking on the phone with your friends," my daughter offered.

"Wrong again."

"You're asking me to get off the phone with mine?"

"Well, sometimes. But the correct answer is that I'm making dinner, and before I can do that, I'm cleaning certain people's stuff off the counter tops and listening to why no one wants the dinner that was posted for the night and changing the menu and discovering I don't have the right ingredients and running to the store to get more and opening the mail and actually making a dinner and putting that dinner on the table and then doing the dishes. And by then it's 8:30, but somebody needs a piece of poster board, and there's no gas in the car. And then, of course, I'm exercising. Intensely. All of which makes me late for bed."

The last entry drew puzzled looks.

"When have you been exercising?"

"Well, if I had been, I would have been even later getting to bed, which would make me a sitting duck for another fifteen pounds or so and probably a heart attack."

When I shared all this with my friend Susan, she added another important piece of information.

"Stress makes you gain weight," she said, "so if you rush around trying to do too much too fast so you can get to bed earlier, it will only make you heavier."

"Of course," I replied, "which is why the Sleep More Plan means you have to do very little."

She said that was exactly in sync with a book she'd read about why French women don't get fat.

"They just walk a lot," she said, "and eat chocolate croissants."

She didn't explain — and I didn't ask — how they had time to walk a lot and still sleep, but we both noticed that eating a chocolate croissant takes almost no time at all.

I hated to share — and so did not — that my friend Barbara was looking terrific by exercising vigorously 45 minutes a day, six days a week for the rest of her life. Her regimen is courtesy of a book called *Younger Next Year for Women*, which says that at a certain age (precisely ours), the body begins to actually decay from lack of exercise, plunging irretrievably into a state of hibernation. Her new routine is an attempt to re-create the spring of her life by tricking her body into thinking that she is an active hunter foraging for food, as animals do in the spring.

I have only started this book and haven't tried the first suggestion. But already I can tell it will help me lose weight. Every time I start reading it, I fall asleep.

Some Days, I'd Rather Be an Aries

I confess. I read my horoscope. Addicted, I search it for insights like a metal detector scouring a playground for shiny dimes. So I was exuberant when I found this treasure the other morning.

"Organization is the key," my horoscope said. "Take the time to preview your day before it happens, anticipating possible obstacles, so you can be prepared with all you need."

Wow. It made me sit back, like that moment a decade ago when I realized that meals would be easier if I bought the ingredients ahead of time.

Maybe life would be simpler if I imagined what would get in the way and stocked up an arsenal.

I read the horoscope to my husband, who is also an Aquarius. "Let's preview our day," I told him, "and anticipate what could go wrong."

"Based on past experience?" he asked.

"Sure," I said, grabbing our calendars. It was a Saturday.

"You have a haircut at 10 and a doctor's appointment at 11. You're working on some computer project in the afternoon, and we have company coming for dinner. I'm meeting a friend for coffee at 9, buying groceries, visiting my mother, writing in the afternoon, getting ready for company. A pretty easy day. What could possibly go wrong?"

"Probably the garbage disposal," he said. It's true. We haven't had company come once in the last 12 years when the garbage disposal hasn't backed up.

"That's just because I clean out the refrigerator for company in case I'd need to open the door while they're here. I'll skip it this time."

"Or possibly another leak," he added.

"Freak accident," I told him. "What are the odds we'd have two massive leaks in three weeks with a nearly new house?"

"What were the odds the first time?"

I had to admit the prospect of dodging another geyser from under the kitchen sink made me nervous, especially since we'd just repaired the basement ceiling from the last time and the kitchen floor looked like a washboard.

"This time, I'll slide a cake pan under the sink and wear rubber-soled shoes. I'd have probably crawled under the sink sooner if I wasn't worried about electrocuting myself. Of course, my mother may still lose her purse."

Purse-o-mania is always possible. Natty at 90, my mom still attempts fashion feats that I decided years ago were beyond me. Like changing purses. She wears white after Memorial Day, navy after Labor Day, a red Vera Bradley bag for casual, fun occasions, a black one for somber ones. All this means finding the bags, dumping the contents and losing something in the shuffle.

"Help! I can't find my purse!" she'll cry, and off I'll go to her assisted living apartment on a search-and-rescue mission. Unfortunately, social occasions tend to bring on these attacks. Last time was the afternoon of her grandson's wedding, when we were already late from the tornado warning.

"No problem," I told my husband. "We simply won't answer the phone."

Of course, we both knew that would never work. What if it was a call that her nitroglycerin was in the missing purse? Or a call from our daughter for her frequent flyer number because she needs to book the last ticket to San Diego to work on an organic farm? (What???) Or a call from our middle son, who's lost his way visiting a friend in Killbuck, Ohio, and needs us to Google him back to the main road?

It is small consolation that all their likely requests would be completely aligned with their horoscopes. My mom (Libra) was to "Say what you want to happen, with whom, how and when." Our daughter (Taurus) was to "listen to your instinct rather than having to hear another, perhaps misguided, person giving you suggestions." And Lost-in-Killbuck (Cancer) was simply operating "like an artist, creating a masterpiece of personal connection."

As for my husband and me, that shiny dime I found turned out to be a grungy old pop-top. From now on, we're switching to Aries: "To keep your routine from becoming a restriction, leave room for surprises, creativity and the possibility of changing your mind."

It's our best hope.

Leash Laws

Speed cleaning. If you'd like a new method besides bagging your overflow and hiding it before company, one resource is http://www.flylady.net, which will fix you up with a cleaning system that makes cleaning an ongoing project. If you don't want cleaning to be an ongoing project, stick with the bags. But quickly write down everything you've bagged and put the list in a safe place. Don't forget where.

Compulsive organizing. When life is chaotic, it helps to rein in what we can control. So go ahead, buy those drawer organizers, put those spices in order, label the pantry shelves. But before you splurge on organizing hardware, consult some books by the organizing pros. Good ones include Julie Morgenstern's *Organizing from the Inside Out* and Karen Kingston's *Clear Your Clutter with Feng Shui.* Marla Dee's *Get Organized the Clear & Simple Way* is a helpful audio book. Find additional organizing resources on my Web site, http://www.PatSnyderOnline.com. Want some hands-on help? The Leash Laws following Chapter 11 clue you in on hiring a professional organizer.

Sleep, blessed sleep. Even if sleeping more doesn't make you lose weight, it can contribute to a more balanced life. Just how much sleep you need for optimum health is an individual question, but the National Sleep Foundation provides a wealth of information to help you analyze your sleep needs and habits and those of your family, online at http://www.sleepfoundation.org.

Birthday reminders. I do believe in remembering birthdays. I really do. One way to celebrate the spirit of Thanksgiving might be to gather from every existing source birthdays of family and friends who should receive a card or a call, create a master list, and enter the dates on the calendar. Failing that, a communal getaway celebration for close personal friends would allow for the exchange of cards, silly hats, and stories, the gift being the getaway.

Going with the flow. There's a lot of truth to the premise that what happens to us is not as important as how we react to it. Whatever your horoscope reading du jour, life will be more balanced if you leave room for surprises, creativity and the possibility of changing your mind. When strong winds come, the branch that bends does not break.

Getaways. Getting away from the home/office/home routine can be magically refreshing. If the cost of airfare and hotel are an issue, try a day trip or stay overnight with a friend or relative. To keep the magic going, learn how to take mini-retreats. An excellent resource for self-led retreat exercises is Rachel Harris's *20-Minute Retreats*.

Chapter Eleven

Stuff and Other Gifts from our Parents

It's inevitable. Parents age and move out of their overstuffed homes, and we "children" help schlep them and their stuff to digs that are easier to maintain and usually have less storage space.

Suddenly, we are endowed with doubles. Two mixers. Two lawn mowers. Two sets of garden tools. And what about that lovely silver hollowware from our late uncle?

Downsizing is the dog that eats up our storage space.

But happily, with all the stuff, they sometimes pass on other gifts. Irreplaceable ones.

Downsizing Parents No Simple Matter

"101 Tips for Organizing Your Life!" "Try Our 25 Top Time-Savers!" The magazine headlines scream at us from the grocery checkout racks.

Hidden deep inside, harder to find than a fugitive in a witness protection program, are the usual answers: Clean closets monthly! Eliminate everything you don't absolutely need! Return everything to its place!

For the editors of these magazines, who undoubtedly live alone in New York City in small expensive one-closet apartments, these articles make sense. They *have* no stuff. Their parents are storing it for them in their basements somewhere in Ohio.

The rest of us clear out the contents of our kids' college dorm rooms just in time to receive the contents of our parents' houses. For us, these simplification tips are about as useful as the three heirloom cocktail tables we are now trying to fit around the grand piano.

It's not that I don't want to believe in easy answers. I'm a sucker for this notion of simplifying your life. I've got the book, the coffee mug and the little daily calendar that tells you how.

It's just that I haven't worked through all the issues this raises in the world of parental downsizing. They rushed at me full force a few months ago. That's when my mom, widowed a year before, decided wisely to sell her three-bedroom house in Florida and move to a one-bedroom apartment near us in Columbus, Ohio.

Like the magazines, she was practical. They said to eliminate everything that was not absolutely necessary. She said: "I won't have room! Take what you need!" She should write for them. It all sounds so simple.

But what does it say about her flour sifter? It's a little rusty, and the handle doesn't turn so well. She does not have room for it in her apartment, and I guess I don't need it. I simply stir dry ingredients with a fork. But maybe my 12-year-old daughter needs to know how to sift. Or my mom needs to teach her. Or the fork isn't such a good idea.

And since I have my own, what about the sewing machine my mom didn't have room for? The one her mother used and that they both taught me to sew on? I don't absolutely need it. I guess.

And what about the box of files my dad maintained from their very first house? The receipts from the caulking he bought in 1957? The letters he sent to *Reader's Digest* challenging them to prove you don't have to be a subscriber to win? I don't absolutely need them, but could I make some kind of collage?

And even though I have my own, what about that complete set of stemware my parents acquired week by week at the local grocery when I was a kid?

How about the wooden salad bowl set they bought in Hawaii, complete with the one small bowl that their old friend Max ruined when he put it in the dishwasher?

The move is complete, and my mom is settled nicely into the more simplified life of a one-bedroom apartment. She has no basement, and her closets are tidy.

My basement, on the other hand, is littered with brown corrugated packing boxes. The tape is stripped off, and the box flaps are bent where I have examined and re-examined the contents. I plan to eliminate everything I don't absolutely need.

Eventually. Maybe. At least by the time I retire.

Maybe General Sherman Could Help Us All

Growing up in Atlanta, I remember the Civil War stories.

"When Sherman came through on his March to the Sea," we were told, "he burned everything. People were running just ahead of him, burying the family silver."

At the time I thought, "How sad! Some folks probably lost track of that silver forever."

Now I know better than to pity them. They were the lucky ones. Today, they are not sitting in their basements wondering how to dispose of a kettle-black, Pyrex-lined, silver-plated casserole server that their mothers tell them would be "just beautiful" if it were finally polished up and used.

"A little elbow grease and you could probably revive it," says mom about mine, then goes on to make one of her more questionable pronouncements.

"There's nothing more satisfying," she says, "than polishing silver."

I have no problems with elbow grease. It works well — with a little Comet — in the bathroom bowl. But my latest satisfaction survey puts polishing silver behind just about everything else. And if I were to draw one of those time maps that matches hours in the day to priorities, it would not show up at all.

"What would I use it for?" I ask about the casserole.

"It's a casserole," she explains patiently. "You display it or use it to entertain. Besides, it was your Aunt Dottie's."

That, of course, is the ringer. There is nothing worse than wrestling with the tarnished left-behinds of the deceased. "Take good care of these," their ghosts seem to say, waving their arms over boxes of blackened treasures. "They were not cheap, and they were very special to me."

Unfortunately, Aunt Dottie, being from Baltimore, did not have the Sherman problem. She had married into the family with all of her silver intact. Worse yet, she had married my uncle, a proficient golfer, who added scores of engraved, silver-plated trays to her collection.

"Never mind the engraving," my mom said when, at 80, she passed them on to me. "You'll just cover that up with some doilies."

Determined to find a guiltless mode of disposal, I explored selling the stuff on eBay and giving the proceeds to my son and his fiancée as a wedding gift "unless," I have told them, "you would rather have the silver." They assured me they would not.

"Not to worry," I said. "With all the baby boomers opening B&Bs, we should be able to unload the casserole, the trays and even the tea service that grandma won at the savings and loan."

But when I took a quick tour of the virtual garage sale, I rushed to the phone.

"Don't be spending this money till you get it," I said. "Silver casseroles are going for $14.99."

A month or so ago, I was excited to see that a local jewelry store was buying silver. I called my son again. "Take it over and you can have the money," I said. Then I called to alert my over-silvered friend Karen, who was also looking for a means of guiltless disposal.

"Don't waste the trip," she said, "unless you've got solid sterling. I went, hauled it all in and had to load it back in the car."

I have since offered it to the crew picking up old furniture and computer monitors for the church garage sale.

"Don't think so," the crew leader said, "but I can't blame you for trying. I've got a load of it in my basement from my first marriage."

Even now, I am hopeful that some reader will step forward and say, "Are you kidding? I have wanted a silver casserole all my life and will polish it weekly and serve Swedish meatballs in it at fancy cocktail parties if you would only give it to me." My mom would be immensely relieved and accompany me to the presentation.

But in the unlikely event that doesn't happen, I am determined to find a creative solution. Perhaps a chemist reading this could propose an inexpensive process that would extract the thin silver veneer from the pot metal and allow it to be presented to an artist's colony somewhere. Perhaps artists could find ways to fashion exquisite black sculptures made from parts and pieces of silver-plated servers. Perhaps the art form would become such compelling Americana that nonprofit corporations could be set up to receive the parts and pieces in exchange for handsome tax deductions.

Or perhaps, if all else fails, a book could be written about the therapeutic effects of silver cleaning, and the pieces could be successfully marketed to Generations X and Y as stress relievers. I can see it now: My mom on *Oprah.*

"There is nothing more satisfying," she would say in her soft southern drawl, "than polishing silver."

There Is No Simple Answer for Us

I'm the first to try butter brickle almond cherry yogurt or a blue hurricane drink with bananas poking out of the foam.

In food and drink, I want options. But please, not in answering machines.

I say this as an expert, being on a first-name basis now with several young clerks in matching polo shirts at my favorite electronics store.

"I need something simple," I tell them, usually on Tuesday evenings. That's when I drop our daughter at piano and head to the return counter with another taped- up box.

"It's for my mom," I explain. "She doesn't see or hear so well, and her arthritis makes it hard to hit the right buttons."

This is a true statement, but like the directions that come with each gizmo, I've omitted a few simple facts.

I've failed to mention, for example, that I am really buying this for myself. That's because when I'm busy, it's easier to leave my mom a message when I'm thinking about it than to remember to call again.

I've also failed to mention that I myself could not program the thing to stop saying it was Sunday at 3 a.m. and that only the piano player had been able to budge it from the "announcement only" setting so that it would take messages at all.

"Do you have anything that's simpler?" I whine. "Something with one mailbox, one announcement, a couple of large, colorful buttons for Play and Delete and a really clear tone quality?"

They point once again to the far end of the store and utter the usual response: "Whatever we have is on Aisle 19."

Aisle 19 is a metal rack of sleek plastic models with small white buttons and small gray numbers and the jazzy square boxes they come in. I look for one that hasn't already ridden around in the trunk of my car till Tuesday and take it to the front.

It's just a Minute Waltz from there to pick up my technical assistant and head once again to my mom's senior citizens apartment building.

"How nice," says Mama, opening the door for the usual procession. "I see you've got another one."

She serves us diet pop, then sits on the couch and squints her eyes in puzzlement as another robotic voice whirs us through the options of days and hours and minutes and mailboxes and ringer sounds.

This one has it right — 8 p.m. Tuesday — but makes a persistent pulsing sound each time a message is left.

"Doesn't bother me anyway," Mama yells above the din. "I'll be sure and know I have a message."

"But what if you're sleeping?"

"Can't hear it from the bedroom," she shouts. "Besides, I like the feel of the receiver."

Like all the others, we try it for a few days. At first, the assistant's friendly voice comes on, on cue, and we leave a message.

By the second day, the robot answers. By the third, it just rings and rings. And by the fourth, Cousin Katherine calls from Florida because when she calls Mama, she just gets music and voices and suspects foul play.

Finally, we call the receptionist at the seniors complex and ask someone to go check. She calls back gaily.

"I'm fine!" Mama says. "Probably just hit the wrong button. But come any time and try another one. It's so much fun to watch."

No-Sizing Is Tougher Than Downsizing

Until last week, I thought I was a pro at downsizing.

After all, eight years ago, I'd moved my mom from her three-bedroom house into a one-bedroom apartment. In the end, I filled an entire dumpster with has-beens and gave the sewing machine to charity.

"It's all a matter of letting go," I told my friends at the time. "You do what you have to do."

Now, it turns out, I passed only the introductory course. Downsizing 101, from house to apartment, pales compared to Downsizing 102, from large apartment to small assisted-living apartment. And Downsizing 102 is nothing compared to the 200-level course, from small apartment to a three-foot wardrobe, nightstand and four dresser drawers in a senior health care center.

Thanks to a series of medical problems, distressing in themselves, we've zipped through the advanced-level courses with dizzying speed and now stand gawking at a pile of irons, microwaves and whistling tea kettles.

"This isn't downsizing. This is no-sizing," I told my husband. "We are down to the basics, and they still won't fit."

It's true. I used to shop for downsized treasures like a smaller computer table or a small TV stand that also housed tons of videos. Now I'm shopping for travel sizes: toothbrushes, mouthwash and nail files that aren't too wide.

I should have listened to my mom. "There's more in here than you think," she used to say, waving her hand toward the walk-in closet, the underbed chests and generous cabinets she'd filled during eight years in a large apartment. "I feel bad for the day you have to clean this out."

"Looks great compared to my place," I'd tell her. I had no idea how true that would be.

In fairness, the overflow in our basement is not entirely my mom's. It includes the contents of our daughter's sophomore year apartment, various antiques from my husband's family, including a desk the size of a billboard, and the heat-sensitive Kodak moments from my childhood that won't fit into the 10' x 10' storage unit without climate control that I grabbed for a month's free rent.

"I'm kind of postponing the problem with the storage unit," I admitted to my husband.

"You'll figure it out," he said, offering to get rid of his dad's bowling ball and a set of golf clubs.

"I don't think that'll do it," I told him, proceeding to list the items that needed a home: one bed (motorized, massaging), one recliner (motorized, heated, massaging), a corner cabinet my cousin insists is "valuable," a curio cabinet that can hold two boxes of curios, a drop-leaf table, two chairs, and 72 inches of hanging clothes.

I didn't even mention the boxes of valuables that had survived the other moves: the sterling tea set my grandma had taken in lieu of back rent from a destitute opera singer, the well-mended Limoges chocolate set, and the Noritake china teacups made in "Occupied Japan."

"I think we're down to the good stuff," I wailed, "and I'm all out of room."

My mom, on the other hand, seems oddly peaceful without all this stuff. She seems content to listen to music on her (now much smaller) CD player, gaze contentedly at the (now much smaller) 8 x 10 portraits of her grandchildren and watch Ellen dance in the afternoon.

"It's a matter of letting go," she says. "You do what you have to do."

Sounds familiar. Only she really means it.

The Gift of Goose

I've never been much of a decorator. Baskets of prairie grass have never adorned our mantel. Neither have Don Quixote statues made of wire.

So friends are puzzled by the recent addition of a 22-inch gray cement goose in St. Paddy's day garb warming herself by our fireplace.

"Your idea?" they ask.

"Oh, no," I rush to explain. "A gift from my mother-in-law."

The explanation prompts a knowing look. Eyes roll.

"Not what you think," I say. But to explain the Gift of Goose, I have to go back to the first time I met Madge Snyder, four days after our wedding. Since my husband's side of the family was in California, we'd decided to marry here and honeymoon there.

"Thanks for coming!" my mother-in-law cried. With that, she gave me a giant bear hug and a kiss on each cheek "to keep it even," she said.

"Yes!" I said. "Thrilled to be here."

She put her hands on my shoulders and searched my eyes with unsettling intensity.

"Do you sometimes say yes," she asked, "when you want to say no?"

"Never," I lied.

"Well, I just read this book," she said, "and I want to be sure."

Whether it came from the famous book on assertiveness training or her much talked-about ESP, she pressed on, bent on lightening up a daughter-in-law she suspected was way too serious about doing too much too well. The tutorial on being a freer spirit started almost immediately.

"I never measure ingredients," she pointed out the first morning at breakfast, "and I love wearing these aprons I've made out of bath towels."

She twirled around in her sneakers, holding out a towel she'd hand-sewn to a bright orange cloth band. At lunch she iced a layer cake with way too much whipped cream. At dinner, she stuck bananas in her ears and danced.

Later when we came with the children, "Mimi," as they called her, passed out Doublemint gum to each grandchild who visited — equal portions to my two from a previous marriage. And she cheered them all on when they scrambled upstairs and threw paper airplanes over the balcony.

Little by little, her influence crept into our household in small, important ways.

"You would be so proud," I called to tell her one day. "I stuck silk geraniums in the houseplants. And everyone thinks they're real!"

I am sure she smiled, looking out the kitchen window at their own courtyard in glorious artificial bloom.

Which brings us back to Goose.

It was the funky beauty of the courtyard that inspired us to send her the garish cement bird that Ohioans were parking on their front porches.

"She can put her in the courtyard, and we can send outfits for every occasion," I told my husband.

"I just LOVE Goose," she called us to say when the bird arrived wearing a yellow slicker for the rainy season. "I even put a little troll doll on her head as an earthquake detector. First sign of a quake, and Troll falls off."

When we arrived for the next visit, it was clear why the quake detector was working so well. Goose was not in the courtyard. She was sitting right on the fireplace hearth in the otherwise elegant living room.

"Oh, my." I said. "You weren't supposed to put her there. She really belongs outside."

"This is where I want her," she said. "Never out of sight."

After Mimi died, Goose continued her vigil at the

California fireplace, still dressed in the bathrobe and curlers she was wearing on Mimi's last day. My father-in-law, a reserved man, seemed to enjoy the reminder of zanier times. So it was not until he died that the question of finding a home for Goose came up.

"Would you like her back?" my sister-in-law wanted to know.

"No!" I said. Effortlessly.

"Of course we would!!!" said our daughter. "She's going right by the fireplace!!!"

"How about the screened porch?" I asked weakly.

She glared. I relented.

Since then, Goose has managed to lighten us up by wearing a flag dress on the Fourth, a red bikini in August, a dreidel dress for Hanukkah and a heart dress for Valentine's Day. She has been a pumpkin for Halloween and a pilgrim for Thanksgiving.

I was once asked if I ever said yes when I wanted to say no. I lied. Sometimes I do. And this time, I'm glad.

Leash Laws

Let's get organized. Believe it or not, there are professional organizers who specialize in helping you downsize your parents. They can even help you downsize your own stuff if you want to spare your family the eventual pain. You can find such a person through the National Association of Professional Organizers (http://www.napo.net). Organizers normally offer a free consultation and estimate for all or part of a job. One benefit of using a professional organizer is emotional distance. The professional can assist more objectively, without triggering old parent-child issues. But if your budget doesn't permit hiring a professional, or your parents resist having a "stranger" help sort through their stuff, not to worry. Enlisting family members for specific tasks and time periods is another option for sharing the work.

Let's store it. Renting a storage unit can make sense when a parent must quickly vacate a home for an uncertain period of hospitalization or recovery. A climate-controlled unit large and comfortable enough to sort through possessions and retrieve them for later donation or sale is ideal. Just be careful not to let the old "out of sight, out of mind" adage come to life here. Set a reasonable time period at the outset and plan your work to meet that goal.

Let's harness technology. With baby boomers aging, online searches increasingly turn up elder-friendly gizmos such as cell phones, answering machines and CD players with larger buttons and numbers. Just be sure the vendor has a liberal return policy in case the device does not hit a homer with mom or dad.

Let's get creative. As for those bygone-era silver trays and tea sets, I confess. I've bumped into no breakthrough suggestions. Readers of my column, instead of offering to take my own silver treasures off my hands, urged me to let them know if I found a place to dump theirs. One tiny tip: community theaters sometimes need silver for their sets. If one in your neighborhood is advertising a production of *Tea and Sympathy*, run – do not walk – to the theater, set in hand, and offer it up. Worked for me. If they want to return it after the performance, no such luck. I've moved to Dubuque, no forwarding address.

Let's picture it. Sentimental heirlooms and monstrosities like our beloved Goose can become treasured display pieces. Or not. If yours is a "not" but you'd like to keep it in the family, send a digital photo and description of the item to other family members, explain that you're in the midst of a "renovation" or "downsizing" project, and offer to ship it to them by a certain date. If you're feeling generous (or desperate), you can offer to pay the shipping or stipulate that the recipient pays. If there are no takers, enjoy the digital photos and donate the item. My late dad's life-size retirement card, signed by co-workers I barely knew, is now a 4x6 print in the file with his glowing personnel reviews.

Let's not go it alone. Dealing with the physical possessions is just one aspect of caring for aging parents. Form or join a support group of local caregivers, or join one of the many online support groups. Find online groups and other resources for caregivers on my web site, http://www.PatSnyderOnline.com.

Chapter Twelve

Your Father and I Have a Date

It's not easy to find "couple" time. If children or aging parents are not underfoot, they're revolving in and out. And most weekends, the only crashing that happens is one shopping cart into another in the Great American Errand-Running Race.

But we keep trying to find ways, whether it's the Friday night (yawn) movies, tango lessons or various versions of an evening out on the town.

Funny how couple time creates its own complications.

Friday Night: An Expensive Nap

Sure, I love a good touchdown and the taste of a hot dog in the stands. But after a couple months of Friday night football, I have to confess: I really come for the noise.

"How about a movie?" my husband asks, hoping to TGIF in some quiet, dark cavern of a theater with reclining red seats.

"Absolutely not," I say.

The thought terrifies.

There is something about a movie with its large surround sound and cushy red seats that knocks me right out at the end of a week. I scrunch up my toes. I pinch the skin on the back of my hand. I take deep cleansing breaths. But it's always the same.

The young couple meets. They exchange words. They exchange significant glances.

My head begins to nod.

Shots ring out. There's a car chase. The couple is veering off the road. They are 15 years older now and have two kids.

"Did I miss something?" I ask.

My husband throws me an icy stare.

It is not new, this Friday night doze. And it is not limited to B movies.

I've slept through Academy Award winners and through reports of gang-style slayings on the 11 o'clock news. Once, I nodded off during a spectacular — I'm told — Oscar Peterson concert at Severance Hall in Cleveland. And the sleep-inducing qualities of chamber music can work their magic on me even on a Sunday.

But movies are the worst. Unlike concerts, which are all sound and no plot, they lend themselves to the morning-after pop quiz at the breakfast table.

"Fell asleep again, Mom?" our daughter asks, throwing her dad a knowing glance.

"Oh, just for a few minutes," I say, feeling all squirmy under the gaze of one who saw the same flick last week. "I got most of it."

"Then what happened after the car chase?" she wants to know. "What happened when they rolled down the hill?"

I freeze, wishing that I had somehow inherited the talent of my dad, a church snoozer, for making up sermons he'd "heard" when I sat in her place years ago and quizzed him over Sunday lunch.

"It was about forgiveness," he would say, with a pointed stare.

I feel lucky by comparison. At least in the movies, the nodding and head-jerking are private. Not visible to 35 Methodists in burgundy robes singing "How Great Thou Art."

"I'm not the only one," I tell her. "I'm sure I'm not the only one who can't make it through a movie."

I am sure of this. I haven't heard many confessions, but the evidence is clear. Video stores are all about not having to wake up and drive home. And at the theater, the whole concession stand business is really about staying awake.

I set out to make my case.

"We pay twice as much for a 'snack' as a ticket," I tell her. "There's not just pop; there's now coffee. And not just coffee, but cappuccino and espresso. The candy bars are as big as shoeboxes, and the popcorn tubs are big enough to bathe a newborn in. All in the hope we won't snore with our mouths full."

She looks unimpressed. "OK, then. So were their kids all right in the end," she wants to know, "after they rolled down the hill?"

I fish for the last couple of Cheerios swimming around in the bowl.

"I'll get to that later," I say, "as soon as the video's out."

Ballroom Puts Dance in Busy Marriage

There was no doubt about it. Life had been hectic, and we needed some quality time. So when I saw the ad for two introductory ballroom dancing lessons, I jumped at the chance to go tango.

"Ten dollars!" I shrieked to my husband. "What a deal!"

Tangoman wasn't sure. "I'm a drummer," he reminded me. "Drummers don't dance."

"Drummers," I reminded him, "have better rhythm than anyone. We will be great!"

The only one not enticed by the mutual flattery that followed was daughter, then 12.

"Where," she wanted to know, "would you be doing this?"

As all parents of preteens should, we answered in unison with the most dreaded response of all: "In public."

She gasped, but we were undeterred.

The first lesson introduced us not only to the tango, but more memorably to a tall, graceful woman we'll call Susan, whose slender ankles wreathed in silver bracelets were arched ballerina-like on tall metallic sandals.

Susan quickly disabused us of the notion that it takes two to tango. Susan led, as I counted and lunged, counted and lunged to the Latin rhythms. Tangoman led as Susan counted and lunged, counted and lunged to the Latin rhythms. Susan stood politely, adjusting the volume on the Latin rhythms as Tangoman and I both led, lunging into each other and rarely counting.

"It just takes practice," she smiled sweetly, and began to instruct us not only on the tango but also on the available options for more lessons, which she recommended if we were to become "socially at ease" with our dancing selves.

She looked gorgeous, I couldn't help but notice. I quickly directed Tangoman to the sign near the coffeemaker, which instructed students not to fraternize with the instructors.

"We are socially at ease," I assured her in the face of a recommended package pricey enough to buy a used car, and I asked Tangoman to dive into his briefcase for a legal pad to scribble down tango instructions, which we promised we would practice at home.

Later that night, when he pulled out the crumpled yellow legal sheets in the bedroom, we struggled to make out the ballpoint pen marks, but to no avail. We put on the tango music, held the paper at arms' length and tried once again to perform what the studio brochure described as the dance with which Rudolph Valentino once wowed the nation.

I had hoped that with just a little more practice, the tango would fulfill its promise to us. Its staccato rhythms were supposed to improve Tangoman's ability to lead and mine to follow — a doubtful scenario, he pointed out, when I had just led him out of the studio.

We've continued to practice, though, lunging into each other, laughing a lot, feeling socially at ease with each other for no additional charge.

Right now, we're having fun with minimal instruction, and if we ever again threaten to go public, I know a 12-year-old eager to babysit around the clock to pay for more lessons.

With this Ring, I'll Eat Jalapenos

With every wedding comes the classic advice: It's not a 50-50 proposition. Each of you will have to give 100 percent.

But few know what this actually means, so let me translate: For the rest of your wedded lives, like it or not, you will be forced to share food.

At the altar, she's asked, "Do you take this man?" But the real question is, "Will you take these brussels sprouts? They're his favorite."

"Do you take this woman?" the officiant wants to know. But if he were honest, he'd add, "With jalapenos? She likes them in everything."

My husband looks up from the menu in a white-cloth restaurant.

"What are you having?" he asks.

"Maybe the pan-seared scallops."

"Oh," he says with a scowl. "I was thinking we could share." Unconsciously, he is scratching his arms as if they've already broken out in shellfish-induced hives.

I scan the menu again, tempted by the calorie-saving, money-saving idea of splitting an entrée or the adventure of ordering two and sampling generously from his plate.

"Uh, maybe the tilapia then," I say, mentally counting the number of little blue packages full of fast-frozen ones in our freezer at home.

"Not if you want the scallops," he protests.

"I love broiled fish," I tell him, pinning an invisible gold star on my collar engraved, "I just gave 100 percent."

"I was thinking I might order broiled chicken and steamed broccoli," says he in a continuing quest for the bland. "Would you eat some of mine?"

"Yes, and how about some shredded wheat with organic rice milk?" I want to say. But I smile.

"Sounds really healthy," I tell him, wishing the chocolate

mousse was not $6.95.

When dinner arrives, he gallantly shares a small forest of broccoli in exchange for my carrots amandine with fresh ginger, which he loathes. Too spicy.

"Interesting," he says.

"I could make them at home," I say.

He glowers. "Maybe not."

Still, I have to admit that even with mismatched tastes, spousal food-sharing has its rewards. Tasting, nibbling and sampling are both the unadvertised perks and curses of marriage.

My friend Nan follows her husband through the potluck line. "Try the beans," she urges, "the ones with the sausage."

"You try them," he says, staring at her veggie-filled plate.

"No," she says. "I'll just taste yours."

And sure enough, while she's sitting in the host's living room munching on celery sticks and carrot chips, her fork migrates to his beans, his fried chicken.

"Doesn't count if it's on his plate," she explains.

Like free samples in a supermarket, spousal food is free — of calories, Weight Watchers points and over-indulgence.

I'm just as guilty.

"Why the shrimp?" my husband asks, staring at the small glass plate I've handed him with cocktail sauce and fat orange tails. "You know I'm allergic."

"Not to worry," I say, retrieving them one by one. "I didn't want to look like a pig."

Eventually, I return to the buffet and grab a new plate, now piled with broiled chicken tenders and broccoli florets. "For my husband," I explain.

Once again, I am wearing an invisible gold star. And so, for his patience, is he.

Home Is Where the Help Is

I read the other day that the latest way to find a babysitter is a match-making process like speed dating. Prospective sitters and desperate couples show up at the same place and rotate through five-minute meetings to get to know each other.

"Check this out," I told my husband. "We should have been so smart. Mass interviews! Disaster prevention!"

"Doubtful," he said. "Who would show up at speed dating smacking Juicy Fruit and wearing a pink wig?"

"Who would show up to babysit like that?" I asked.

He just looked at me, and then I remembered: the pink-haired lady who had been "screened" by a professional agency. Cotton Candy, we called her. She had come to us on a day of desperation when we each had a meeting we believed was more important than the other's and the boys had strep throat.

"Some screening process *they* had," he said.

"Some screening process *we* had," I said. Because the truth is, no amount of interviewing ever guaranteed a no-surprise experience when it came to babysitters.

Still, we persisted on the advice that even after children, marriage must come first. Evenings out must continue. Romance is meant to linger.

We just hope ours lingers for as long as the babysitter stories. With the youngest already in college, the tales persist.

"I can't work Sundays," one work-week sitter told us. No problem, we said. Then we jumped back when we found religious tracts she'd left us, on the evils of working mothers.

A young woman who assured us she worked well without direction volunteered to do odd jobs around the house when the kids were napping.

"A self-starter!" I told my husband. Imagine our surprise when we discovered she'd re-touched our glossy white kitchen cabinets with a basting brush and some leftover wall paint.

Naturally, we avoided sitters the children couldn't stand,

but we soon learned to be more skeptical of the ones they really liked. That wisdom came with a woman we'll call Sabrina, a 15-year-old who took it upon herself to give the boys piano lessons and, more significantly, sneaked her family's cable box in her purse and hooked up the TV — and our boys — with movies that would make Walt Disney blush.

"Can she please come again?" the children would ask with uncharacteristic enthusiasm for a musical education. When we noticed that the C scale had been inked indelibly on the ivories, the oldest even took full credit to keep her from being fired.

"Sorry," he sniveled on the way up to his room.

For awhile, it was heaven. With such a popular sitter, we went out nearly every weekend. Sadly, one night the cable box spilled out of her handbag and, soon, the full story.

"We need a more mature sitter," I announced, going on to hire a white-haired woman complete with bun.

"I feel better already," I told my husband as we pulled out of the driveway. Sure enough, there were no calls for help, but we had to shake her awake when we got home.

As she snored, our older one, almost the age of Sabrina and hungry for money, made his pitch that he could provide more vigilance. As he pointed out, it had been several years since he locked his brother in the closet. And the night the younger one installed a discarded toilet on the neighbors' front stoop? Well, we'd been in charge then and slept right through.

"OK," we said, as he cleverly proposed a better rate than we'd paid Cotton Candy or Sleepy, and soon we went out for an evening at a restaurant very nearby.

Again, no calls for help. And when we called to check on them every seven minutes or so, no complaints. When we got home, the dishes were done, there was no sign of a struggle and the "sitter" looked extraordinarily clean-cut.

"Fine job!" my husband said.

"Excellent!" said I, trying to be discreet as I peeked at the piano keys, just to make sure.

Leash Laws

Friday night date? Give it up. Why do you think every other car on Friday night is delivering pizza? After a high-speed week, the truly ambitious empty a salad bag, speed-dial Domino's and set the table. Saturday is another story. Going out somewhere, sans kids, is an important break, even if your budget permits just packing a picnic and trading off babysitting with another couple. (No, comatose babysitting on Friday night does not count as a trade).

Lessons. Whether it's learning to dance, cook Mexican, or play the kazoo, lessons are great bonding experiences for couples. Sometimes, the less expert you become, the better. These shared experiences give you something to laugh and talk about besides religion, politics and a national health care plan.

El cheapo fun. Cooking parties and potlucks can make for fun and inexpensive couples' entertaining, too. An easy way to host a cooking party is to distribute a menu and recipes ahead and have each couple bring the ingredients. Better yet, let the menu itself be a surprise by letting each couple choose a recipe and bring ingredients to make it. It's easy on the budget and something to talk about besides global warming and a national energy policy.

Sharing. "What's up with this food-sharing?" some readers asked after my column ran about couples sharing food. They introduced me to a new concept that I call "pre-emptive ordering." That is, a vegetarian and a carnivore walk into a restaurant. The carnivore orders pasta with meat sauce and a salad laced with pepperoni. The vegetarian orders tofu, which the carnivore has never tasted but does not like. Voila! Total food-sharing protection for both.

Sib sitting. It's worth a try when the one left in charge is mature and has had the safety training you'd expect from an outside sitter, and there's a healthy relationship between sibs. A trial run with the parents just down the street at a neighbor's could be a good start. In any case, it's up to the parents to set ground rules that are understood by everyone involved.

About The Author

For nearly a decade, Pat Snyder, a lawyer and mother of three, has chronicled her crazed struggle to lead a balanced life in "Balancing Act," a regular humor column that appears in Suburban News Publications, a chain of 22 weekly papers in the Columbus, Ohio, area.

When she is not dancing around in a Dr. Seuss hat and leading laugh-ins as a certified laughter leader with the World Laughter Tour (http://www.worldlaughtertour.org), Pat, an award-winning writer, speaks on life balance and leads workshops to help others bring more humor into their lives and their writing.

Before law school, she worked as a reporter for the *Akron Beacon Journal.* When her marriage to the late Bob Snyder made him both an unsuspecting stepparent and first-time parent, the two of them co-authored a Sunday column for *The (Cleveland) Plain Dealer* on the challenges of stepfamily living. Her account of their adventures combining his Hanukkah traditions with her Christmas ones was published in the book *Cup of Comfort for Christmas.*

Pat lives in Columbus, Ohio, with all the dogs that eat her planner. Her online home is http://www.PatSnyderOnline.com.

Acknowledgments

Much quoted in *The Dog* are those who fueled my personal balancing act even before I began writing a newspaper column by the same name. They are my late husband Bob Snyder, my late mom Polly Ondo, and children Paul Ravenscraft, James Ravenscraft and Sarah Snyder. Thanks for your humor, your patience and especially for not rolling your eyes too often when your antics appeared in print.

Bouquets also ...

For ongoing support to Jim Toms, the publisher of Suburban News Publications, who encouraged me to write the "Balancing Act" column a decade ago "if you can find enough material" and cheered me on during the writing of this book.   Also, to the SNP commentary editors who edited the column over the years: Cliff Wiltshire (now managing editor), Shelly Coffman, Bill Melville, Lyndsey Teter and Garth Bishop.

For their technical support and creativity, to Mark Levine of Two Harbors Press, along with book editor Matthew Dewald and cartoonist Michael H. Whiting.

For their expertise on laughter and humor, to joyologist Steve Wilson, founder of the World Laughter Tour and Tim Bete, former director of the Erma Bombeck Writers' Workshop.

For their steady emotional support, to the women of my Visioning Group (including Mary Christensen, Barbara McVicker, Leslie Robinson and Amy Ryan Rued) and Writers' Night Out (including Shannon Jackson Arnold, Lora Fish, Nancy Golden, Shirley Hyatt, Lynn McNish and Nita Sweeney).

And finally, for their enthusiasm and suggested "leash laws," the readers of "Balancing Act."